Inheriting the Master's Cloak

JOHN
WIJNGAARDS, MHM

Inheriting the Master's Cloak

CREATIVE BIBLICAL SPIRITUALITY

AVE MARIA PRESS NOTRE DAME, INDIANA 46556

Scripture quotations in this book are from the *Good News Bible,* the
Bible in Today's English Version. Copyright © American Bible Society,
1976. Used by permission.

_____

© 1985 by John Wijngaards, MHM
All rights reserved.

International Standard Book Number: 0-87793-287-5 (cloth)
0-87793-288-3 (paper)

Library of Congress Catalog Card Number: 85-71535

Cover and text design: Katherine A. Robinson
Printed and bound in the United States of America.

To my charming and capable
Housetop colleagues
Jackie Clackson, Simone Donnelly
and Anne Miller
with thanks for their
advice and unfailing support

Contents

Introduction: Strangers at the Door of My Tent / 11

Part One: The God of the Old Covenant

1 Escape From the Cannibal God / 21
2 Finding the Culprit for Famine and Plague / 31
3 Give and Take in a Pact of Love / 39
4 Refusing Pork — and Make-believe / 49
5 Building a Home for a Traveling Spirit / 57
6 Pouring Perfume on Tired Feet / 65
7 Fixing Our Gaze Beyond the Known Horizon / 73
8 Ancient Prophets on My Mountain / 83

Part Two: Making the Most of Reading and Prayer

9 Munching Words, Digesting Images / 91
10 Blind Guides That Swallow Camels / 97
11 Welcome to the King of Glory / 107
12 Light for Distant Nations / 117
13 Flowers, Cedars and Mustard Trees / 127
14 Adrift on the Deluge of Living / 133

Part Three: Roots of Christian Discipleship

15 Standing With Two Feet on God's Soil / 145
16 Prophets and Witnesses of Our Master / 151
17 Getting a Donkey Back on Its Feet / 159
18 A Royal Envoy That Was Spat Upon / 169
19 The Word That Makes People a People / 177
20 Storing Treasures That Rapture the Mind / 185

Introduction

Strangers at the Door of My Tent

The Old Testament can be a source of continuous inspiration in our spiritual life. It offers endless scope for widening our spiritual horizon. It deals with aspects of life which are not mentioned in the gospels or the letters of the apostles. In fact, it is four times as voluminous as the New Testament. Many Old Testament texts are presupposed in the New, so we really need to know them for understanding the gospel. In spite of all these good reasons, many people are not on intimate terms with the Old Testament. They find it foreign and bizarre. Just ask them what they think about the Old Testament and they are likely to give you a blunt answer!

"The Old Testament is strange. It requires reams of commentary and explanation. It's too remote from my life."

"There are so many ugly episodes in the Old Testament; too much violence; too many unsavory texts."

"It all happened so long ago! How does it affect me? I prefer books written today."

"Will the time I'll devote to it really pay off? I find all I need in the New. Why bother about the Old?"

Let us admit that our misgivings about the Old Testament are usually more emotional than rational. Intellectually we may be convinced. What is lacking is a feeling of attraction, the experience that the old Testament can inspire us. "Strangeness," "ugliness" and "irrelevance" are affective notions; they describe

11

relationships. Most people associate close and familiar with friendly, beautiful and relevant. A dilapidated house may still be "home sweet home" for the person living in it. Judgments are greatly influenced by feelings. And so it is our feelings we should be talking about.

Consider the example of Ruth. She was a woman from the country of Moab who married an immigrant Jew. When her husband died, her mother-in-law decided to go back to her native land, Israel. Ruth had never been outside Moab. She would find it hard to settle in Israel whereas in her own country she might easily find a new husband. So Naomi, her mother-in-law, urged her: "Why come with me? Stay with your own people." What went on in Ruth's mind and heart? Certainly, no love was lost between the people of Moab and the Israelites. The Israelites would never forget how King Mesha of Moab had massacred 7,000 of their people "as a pleasing sacrifice to his god, Kemosh." They had made it a rule that no Moabite, even if resident in Israel for 10 generations, could become a member of God's people. What sympathy could Ruth expect in such a hostile nation? But she loved her mother-in-law and decided to take the risk. "Don't ask me to leave you. Let me go with you. Your people will be my people; your God will be my God."

Our spiritual life will only grow and mature if we are willing to strike out into unknown territory. We have to break out of the circle of close acquaintances. We have to free ourselves from our exaggerated fear of what is strange. What would have happened to us if we had always remained enclosed within the protected circle of our family and neighbors? Have we not made many exciting and lifelong friends when we broke free by going to school, starting a new job or moving into a new neighborhood? Some of our best friends may have come into our lives through chance meetings. They may be all the more valuable to us because they are different, because their family background or temperament seems just the opposite of what we ourselves would have thought congenial and acceptable.

Ruth was rewarded for her courage. She followed Naomi into a strange country to settle in Bethlehem, a town in which she knew no one. But there she met, and eventually married, a wealthy and kind man called Boaz. Through this marriage she became the great-grandmother of David and ultimately one of the ancestral parents of Jesus himself. Sometimes our greatest opportunities lie where we least expect them!

The Way and the Truth

Perhaps you will say, "But Ruth had Naomi to guide her. Naomi introduced her to her new surroundings." Certainly. But we have Christ. With him we may confidently enter the unfamiliar world of the Old Covenant.

What did Jesus think about Old Testament texts that are full of violence, that are unsavory and crude? He knew exactly how to deal with them. He either left them alone or corrected them explicitly when needed.

> "You have heard that it was said, 'An eye for an eye, and a tooth for a tooth' [from Ex 21:24; Dt 19:21]. But now I tell you: do not take revenge on someone who wrongs you. If anyone slaps you on the right cheek, let him slap your left cheek too" (Mt 5:38-39).

Jesus knew that there were many imperfections in the Old Testament. He accepted this as a matter of fact. Yet he loved the Old Testament. He derived many values of his kingdom from its teaching. Jesus overlooked many of the ugly traits because they were part of a face that was dear to him.

This is the way Jesus read the Old Testament, the way he expects us to read it. The Pharisees and scribes lacked precisely that vision.

> "You study the Scriptures, because you think that in them you will find eternal life. And these very Scriptures speak about me! Yet you are not willing to come to me" (Jn 5:39-40).

> "This people will listen and listen, but not understand; they will look and look, but not see" (Mt 13:14).

> "How terrible for you, teachers of the Law! You have kept the key that opens the door to the house of knowledge; you yourselves will not go in, and you stop those who are trying to go in!" (Lk 11:52).

The problem with the scribes was that they clung to a very narrow and literalistic interpretation of the Old Testament. They could not see how an ancient passage could carry a dynamic, new message. Consider the time they accused Jesus' disciples of picking ears of corn on the Sabbath.

Greater Than David,
More Sacred Than the Temple

Harvesting was one of the activities listed by the scribes as forbidden on the Sabbath. Even picking two ears of corn amounted to a full transgression. I imagine that one of the scribes or Pharisees raised his voice in the ensuing argument and shouted: "What you are doing is forbidden by the Word of God!" At this moment Jesus became silent and thoughtful. He was extremely sensitive to the Word of God. The exclamation challenged him, forced him to consider what the scriptures had to say about the point at issue. Jesus allowed the Old Testament texts to pass through his mind. Two passages spoke to him convincingly, and he answered:

> "Have you never read what David did that time when he needed something to eat? He and his men were hungry, so he went into the house of God and ate the bread offered to God. This happened when Abiathar was the High Priest. According to our Law only the priests may eat this bread— but David ate it and even gave it to his men" (Mk 2:25-26).

> "Or have you not read in the Law of Moses that every Sabbath the priests in the Temple actually break the Sabbath law, yet they are not guilty? I tell you that there is something here greater than the Temple!" (Mt 12:5-6).

The manner in which Jesus uses these texts is very instructive. First of all, notice how he sees them in a new light. David, God's elected servant who was meant to become the ancestor of the Messiah, was in danger of death. Saul's soldiers were on his heels. David and his men might die of hunger. To save their lives the High Priest took the extraordinary step of handing over the sacred loaves to David, loaves that had been dedicated to God and thus had become God's exclusive property. Preserving David was more pressing, more sacred a need than observing a ritual law. The same situation, Jesus sees, applies to himself. He is the Messiah, the awaited Son of David. If his disciples are hungry the same exception from the Law applies to them. Moreover, if the priests are permitted to work in the Temple in spite of the Sabbath because the Temple requires such service, the same tolerance should be extended to those who work in the service of the kingdom. For Jesus, these texts teach that the welfare of God's servants and service for the kingdom are higher values and weightier priorities than conformity to law. But there is more that we can learn. The story of David which Jesus quotes has its crude elements. The 85 priests serving in the Temple and the whole population of Nob were killed by Saul in punishment for the help given to David.

> Saul also had all the other inhabitants of Nob, the city of priests, put to death: men and women, children and babies, cattle, donkeys and sheep—they were all killed (1 Sm 22:19).

Jesus ignores this side of the story. He does not approve of it. He does not draw inspiration from it. He simply accepts it as an aspect of the ancient, imperfect covenant. He knows only too well that revelation unfolded itself through human language and thus bears the imprint of its human history.

Thirdly, and this is truly amazing, Jesus quotes the Davidic episode inaccurately. He says: "This happened when Abiathar was the High Priest." But in 1 Samuel, chapter 21 we read that it was Ahimelech who gave David the sacred bread to eat! Abiathar was Ahimelech's son. He escaped from the massacre and became High Priest at a later date. So Jesus gave the credit to the wrong High Priest! Some commentators feel embarrassed about this and suggest that the mention of Abiathar may be due to a later interpolation or to an oversight on the part of the evangelist. I don't understand their anxiety. In fact, I find it consoling and worthy of meditation to take the text as it stands and to make Jesus himself responsible for the inaccuracy. Jesus was quoting from memory, after all, and nothing was more natural than for him to make such a slip, especially because Abiathar was so prominent in David's life during a later period. The comfort I derive from this mistake on Jesus' part is that it shows categorically that the historical detail itself was of no consequence. Whether Abiathar or Ahimelech was High Priest at the time was not a matter about which Jesus was concerned. His mistake teaches us with unmistakable authority that we too should read the Old Testament texts (and the New Testament ones for that matter) with our attention focused on the central message, not on historical detail.

The Old Testament books are very human. They show this human characteristic in the style of writing, in frequent neglect of exact reporting, in prejudiced views and attitudes, in a slowly developing appreciation of who God is and what he wants. Though written under inspiration, they could not be more human than they are. It is good to be aware of the fact that this human (and therefore imperfect) quality did not stop Jesus from finding inspiration and guidance in the old texts.

A Path of New Awareness

Indeed, the way Jesus used the Old Testament texts can lead us to a path of new awareness. Jesus will help us discover exciting values and precious openings we never knew of. His enthusiasm will open our eyes as it opened the eyes of the two disciples on the way to Emmaus.

> Then Jesus said to them: "How foolish you are, how slow you are to believe everything the prophets said! Was it not necessary for the Messiah to suffer these things and then to enter his glory?" And Jesus explained to them what was said about himself in all the Scriptures, beginning with the books of Moses and the writings of all the prophets (Lk 24: 25-27).

I am always struck in this text by the word *all* in the phrase "all the Scriptures." The early Christians kept collections of favorite texts culled from various Old Testament books. Luke says, in effect, that a comprehensive list of that nature went back to Jesus himself. Jesus had a way of reading the Old Testament that was personal and unique.

How interesting it would have been for us if we could have been there, listening to Jesus quoting and explaining the Old Testament. Surely, Jesus was not referring to these texts merely for the sake of argument, to furnish rabbinical proofs as it were. No, the Old Testament scriptures were his Father's words to him and he undoubtedly spoke of them with enthusiasm. Listening to Jesus might have cured us in one stroke of our doubts and misgivings. We could not have failed to catch some of his interest and excitement.

Taking the Old Testament seriously is like undertaking a new journey. We move into unknown territory, ready to encounter new friends among strangers, our eyes open for what God is going to show us. If this is the spirit in which we take up our Old Testament reading, we will be surprised at the spiritual profit it will bring us. The purpose of this book is to give you the "feel" of what your journey could be like. I am talking to you as a fellow-traveller, pointing out routes I found useful myself, sharing some of the experiences I had on the way. I hope and pray that the insights I have received and the exhilaration I feel may somehow rub off on you, may prove contagious so that you will joyfully start your own explorations. Part of the way we can walk together. Afterward you will have found your feet. You will then go forward with confidence.

Though God is ready to give us great gifts, he does occasionally wait for us to make the first move. Let us call to mind that remarkable story of the three strangers who were Abraham's guests.

> As Abraham was sitting at the entrance of his tent during the hottest part of the day, he looked up and saw three men standing there. As soon as he saw them, he ran out to meet them. Bowing down with his face touching the ground, he said, "Sirs, please do not pass by my home without stopping; I am here to serve you. Let me bring some water for you to wash your feet; you can rest here beneath this tree. I will also bring a bit of food; it will give you strength to continue your journey. You have honored me by coming to my home, so let me serve you."
>
> They replied, "Thank you; we accept" (Gn 18:1-5).

The story continues to describe Abraham's hospitality: how he made Sarah bake new bread, how he prepared a fatted calf, how he served the meal himself, with milk and cream. Abraham did not know it, but God himself was one of the three guests. Toward the end of the visit God blessed the home with the promise that Abraham and Sarah would have their own son—something they had prayed for during their whole lives.

We said at the beginning of this chapter that the Old Testament texts may at first give the impression of being ugly, strange and irrelevant. Could they be the three strangers standing in front of our tent during the hottest part of the day?

—————————————— Part One

The God
of the
Old Covenant

"You spoke a word
and my world came to be.
You molded me from clay.
You walked in the evening breeze.
You proclaimed your Law for me
with thunder and lightning
on Mount Sinai.
You were throned between cherubim
on the covenant ark;
and struck down Uzzah
when he dared to touch it....

"Who are you
El Shaddai,
Elohim Adonai,
Yahweh Sabaoth?"

"I am the One
whom Jesus called his Father.
I am the Glory,
the Light,
full of mercy and compassion,
slow to anger,
abounding in love."

1

Escape From the Cannibal God

The Old Testament recounts quite a number of atrocities. For me, one of the most horrible incidents is narrated as part of a war between Israel, Judah and Edom on the one side, and Moab on the other. The three armies had invaded Moab, had driven the Moabites back to their capital Kir Heres and were laying a siege round that city. The king of Moab was desperate. He tried to break out with the pick of his troops, but failed. Finally he made a vow to Chemosh, promising the god his eldest son in return for victory.

> So he took his oldest son, who was to succeed him as king, and offered him on the city wall as a sacrifice to the god of Moab (2 Kgs 3:27).

What a terrifying picture! A father killing his own child in the belief that this would please his god! A cruel god, he must have considered him, a god who would only be satisfied by blood, by the life of his own child. An ugly story, which we might want to read over in a hurry, or simply forget. But I believe it is worth a lot of reflection. And reflecting on its implications we may also discover that the so-called "ugly traits" of the Old Testament may have more meaning than we suspected.

The king of Moab sacrificed his son. That is bad enough. But far worse—I would almost say incomprehensible—is the fact that child sacrifice was a common practice among the Israelites too. When Jericho was rebuilt in 860 B.C., Hiel, its mayor, offered his eldest son, Abiram, for the laying of the foundations and his youngest son, Segub, when building the gates. Excavations at Shechem have shown the remains of small children under the city gates. Jephthah of Gilead killed his only daughter in fulfilment of a vow. Outside Jerusalem, in the valley of Hinnom, sacrificing children was done on a regular basis.

It is difficult to reconstruct exactly how frequently sacrifices were conducted. But from the available evidence, we may piece the parts together in the following scene. In the valley of Hinnom, hardly 15 minutes' walk from the Temple precinct, was a sanctuary to Melek on a small hill called Topheth. We may presume that people would vow to sacrifice their children to obtain certain favors. When the time for the sacrifice came, people would gather in the open compound of the sanctuary, where they would face the statue of the god. From ancient writers we know that it must have looked like a standing bronze figure. Inside, the figure was hollow, so that it could serve as a furnace. There was probably a hole at the back of the pedestal so that a fire could be lit that would make the whole statue red hot. People would dance and sing. Then the child would be taken from its mother's arms. Sometimes it may have been stabbed to death; at other times it may have been offered alive. In both cases the body of the child was put on the outstretched arms of the idol, arms that were red hot. Possibly there was a hole in the belly of the idol, too, so that the child would slide or roll down along the arms to disappear into the fire inside. We may well imagine hearing the screams of the child—and its mother!

This practice endured for at least four centuries. When Solomon turned to the worship of foreign gods he built the shrine to Melek at Topheth (950 B.C.). A hundred years later the deuteronomistic lawgivers complain:

> Do not worship the LORD your God in the way they worship their gods, for in the worship of their gods they do all the disgusting things that the Lord hates. They even sacrifice their children in the fires on their altars (Dt 12:31).

Again, a hundred years later, we read how King Ahaz (736-716 B.C.) also followed this practice:

> He even sacrificed his own son as a burnt offering to idols, imitating the disgusting practice of the people whom the LORD had driven out of the land as the Israelites advanced (2 Kgs 16:3).

Of King Manasseh (687-642 B.C.) the same is said (2 Kgs 21:6). Fifty years later the prophet Jeremiah has this to say:

> In Hinnom Valley they have built an altar called Topheth,
> so that they can sacrifice their sons and daughters in the
> fire (Jer 7:31).
>
> They have built altars to Baal in Hinnom Valley, to sacrifice
> their sons and daughters to the god Molech (Jer 32:35).

The sanctuary was destroyed by King Josiah (640-609 B.C.) in his
sweeping reforms:

> King Josiah also desecrated Topheth, the pagan place of
> worship in Hinnom Valley, so that no one could sacrifice
> his son or daughter as a burnt offering to the god Molech
> (2 Kgs 23:10).

Yet 50 years later Ezekiel still speaks about it:

> "You took the sons and daughters you had borne me and
> offered them as sacrifices to idols. Wasn't it bad enough to
> be unfaithful to me, without taking my children and sacrific-
> ing them to idols?" (Ez 16:20-21).

The abominable practice at Topheth was like an incurable disease.

The Cruel God

Why? I have often asked myself. Why this unbelievable cruelty? Did parents not love their children? They did, as much as
parents today love theirs. Jephthah's heart was broken when he
offered his daughter. Yet he killed her! What was stronger than
his pity and his sorrow? What was it that made generation after
generation go to Topheth to see their children's flesh singe in the
arms of Melek? What power did Melek, that flaming monster,
hold over people?

Perhaps I saw the answer in Tirupathi in the south of India.
Hundreds of thousands of pilgrims go there every year to redeem
vows made to Venkateshwara. They go the last miles up into the
Tirumala hills on foot. They take a bath in the holy pond, then
pay a visit to the idol itself. Ten feet high it stands, with its dark
and ugly face, that mask of cruelty and silent anger. Looking at
the idol I shuddered. I felt I stood face to face not with God, but
with a parody of divinity, with the cruel, relentless, heartless
avenger-god we have made of him. Outside the temple in the
barbers' hall I watched in horror and fascination as women had
their beautiful hair cut off. I remembered that offering one's hair
became a substitute for human sacrifice; an improvement, no

doubt, but retaining the same cruel streak of destroying something beautiful belonging to oneself.

The child-sacrifices to Melek, the pilgrimages to Lord Venkateshwara, the worship of the goddess Kali, are like a bad dream to me. They bring out something very deep from my subconscious. How shall I give expression to it in words? I believe God is good, yet deep down inside me is an unspoken, unreasonable fear of him. The fear is this: One day or another he will extract a terrible price for his goodness. One day or another he will make me suffer, make me lose something I hold precious. He is, after all, God, and I am nothing. If I am lucky, he will not take everything; he will leave me at least part of what I treasure. That is why, if I am a woman, I may offer him my flowing tresses, so that he may allow me to keep the health of my children. If I were an Israelite, I might be prepared to sacrifice my beloved child to him to preserve the lives of the rest of the family. But if I am enjoying life and the good things he has given me, I feel an unease deep within myself, in the pit of my stomach, for I know he has not yet struck and made me pay the price.

This human fear, which I am sure every religious person has to face, was present in Israel too. With them, it was a collective fear. It was a fear that naturally arose from paternalistic authority structures and from the ancient covenant's stress on curse and punishment. The god Melek, that cruel brass monster that stretched out its arms to grab children and swallow them in its fiery belly—what else is it but an archetype of the hardness projected onto God? And archetypes, we know from Jung, crop up in our dreams and may have a healing function.

God is not a monster. He did not want human sacrifice, as prophets and lawgivers pointed out time and again:

> "Don't sacrifice your children in the fires on your altars....The LORD your God hates people who do these disgusting things" (Dt 18:10,12).

> "They have built altars for Baal in order to burn their children in the fire as sacrifices. I never commanded them to do this; it never even entered my mind" (Jer 19:5).

> "If anyone gives one of his children to Molech and makes my sacred Tent unclean and disgraces my holy name, I will turn against him and will no longer consider him one of my people" (Lv 20:3).

The language is unusually emotional in all these texts. The practice is disgusting; it makes God's sanctuary unclean; it disgraces God's name. God hates people who act thus. The thought of wanting human sacrifice never even entered God's mind! In other words, the practice springs from humankind itself, from confused thinking, from distorted ideas of what God wants. The practice could not be uprooted by threats and punishments — as history bears out — it could only be uprooted by a healing in people's minds.

Bloodthirsty Redemption

Psychology tells us that dreams can heal, if they are properly understood and if their contents are faced with honesty. The monster Melek should not be suppressed in our dreams; it should be faced and confronted. Is Melek my God? Is it he I fear and worship in the hidden anxiety of my subconscious? Why does he have a hold on me? What is the cause of my fear, or my distorted vision of God? Am I projecting onto him my experiences of unexpected loss and suffering? Am I attributing to God traits of cruelty and vindictiveness I have seen in my parents or other authority figures of my childhood? What are the bits and pieces of my early experiences that have helped to build up my concept of God? Are there feelings, perhaps, that need to be adjusted in the light of my later understanding of God? If we examine these questions sincerely, they will gradually reveal aspects of our religious life we may never have been aware of. As we begin to recognize the place of Melek in our emotions and our subconscious mind, we can extricate ourselves in stages from his stranglehold.

The process of healing may also involve a better understanding of Christian theology. There have been theologians in the past who have constructed a theory of redemption which is not much better than a baptized version of Melek doctrine. Their presentation of the history of salvation could be expressed in terms such as these: Mankind had sinned. God was looking for a way to redeem us from this sin, but his strict sense of justice had to be satisfied first. In other words, God could not simply forgive sins through an act of mercy; satisfaction had to be offered to his justice. God decided to solve the problem by making his own Son assume human nature and die a violent death. Through his bloody sacrifice Christ paid the price on behalf of all. Only then could

God forgive sins and receive us back as his children.

The origins of this theology lie in the Middle Ages. The word *justice*—used in St. Paul's letters—was understood in legal terms, not in the sense of "making holy" intended by Paul (see Rom 3:21-26). It misunderstood the notion of vicarious suffering expressed in Deutero-Isaiah and applied to Jesus (Is 52:13—53:12). It gave a wrong meaning to the way in which Jesus' death is said to be the will of the Father (Mt 26:36-43) and misrepresented what Peter said about Jesus "having paid the price" (1 Pt 1:18-19). It is not difficult to see how all these texts, if not properly understood, could lead to the theory mentioned above. All the more so if the unconscious concept of God accepted by these theologians was somewhat tainted by the "Melek" syndrome!

Grace and Free Gift

The theological construction above is wrong, first of all, because the idea of human sacrifice giving God satisfaction goes contrary to what scripture teaches about God. "Such an idea never entered my mind!" we read in Jeremiah three times. How could we expect God the Father to do to his beloved Son what he abhorred in the parents of Israel? Secondly, redemption would become a deal instead of being a free act of mercy. The point of the salvation brought through Jesus is precisely that it is a free gift of God the Father, not based on wages of any sort. Thirdly, if Jesus' death on Calvary were the price which he paid to satisfy his Father's justice, why was his resurrection equally important for redemption? If Jesus' death were the sacrifice that satisfied his Father's anger, we would have been saved also without the resurrection. Yet without the resurrection, St. Paul tells us, "your faith is a delusion and you are still lost in your sins" (1 Cor 15:17).

How then should redemption be understood? Jesus, the only-begotten Son, the Word of God, became a human being. He brought us grace and truth, because no one had ever seen God, but he had. He made the Father known. And to those who believed in him, he gave the right to become God's children. From an analysis of John 1:1-18 it is clear that Jesus saved us by a gift of his life. He saved us by becoming man and by extending his own life to those who joined him in faith. A similar picture emerges from reading that other summary of Jesus' salvific function in the high-priestly prayer of John 17.

Not My Will But Yours Be Done

What then about Jesus' death and resurrection? Jesus' crucifixion was a crime. Jesus calls it a sin and repeatedly protests his innocence. In that sense it was not willed by God and could not be willed. But for Jesus to be true to his mission, he had to stand by his disciples to the end. He was not like the hired shepherd who runs away in the face of danger. He was ready to die for his sheep. This readiness of Jesus to die was pleasing to his Father; in that sense it was the Father's will.

"The Father loves me because I am willing to give up my life, in order that I may receive it back again" (Jn 10:17).

Jesus' death, which resulted from hatred and sin, became, in fact, the highest expression of his human love. The greatest love a person can show is to give up life itself for another. That is why God chose it to become the turning point in Jesus' redemptive life. Just as the passover sacrifice marked the Exodus and the old covenant, so Jesus' death was seen as the sacrifice marking our exodus from sin and the conclusion of the new covenant. Jesus' resurrection inaugurated our new existence under direction of the Spirit (Jn 14:15-31).

The song of the "suffering servant," Is 52:13—53:12, which was so important for Jesus and the early church in explaining his death and resurrection, confirms this interpretation. An innocent man is condemned to death. He suffers terribly. But he is a special person because he lives and prays for others. That is why God decides to use this suffering to bring forgiveness:

"It was my will that he should suffer;
    his death was a sacrifice to bring forgiveness....
After a life of suffering he will again have joy;
    he will know that he did not suffer in vain....
He willingly gave his life
    and shared the fate of evil men.
He took the place of many sinners
    and prayed that they might be forgiven" (Is 53:10,11,12).

But Jesus' suffering was preordained by God, you may object. Isaiah 53:10 states: "It was my will that he should suffer!" And in Gethsemane Jesus clearly accepts suffering and death only because it is his Father's will. Thus the Father wanted Jesus to die in order to make his death the sacrifice for all.

Yes, it was the Father's will, and yet, it wasn't! How is this explained? It was not the Father's will in the sense that he wanted that death itself, as something determined by his absolute will. As we have seen, he could not want it like that because it involved a sin. And God cannot contradict himself by wanting an evil thing. But when the option of death faced Jesus as a consequence of being faithful to his mission, then the Father wanted it. Because he wanted Jesus to be faithful.

Suppose a young man joins the army. He attains the rank of lieutenant. War breaks out. He hears that he may be sent to the front line in the near future. In those circumstances he writes his father this letter:

> "Dear Dad: When I left home both you and Mother asked me to look after myself and not to risk my life without need. I know they will ask for volunteers from among the officers to lead the next infantry attack. I feel it may be my duty to volunteer, even though it will expose me to enemy fire. What do you want me to do? Should I die for my country?"

I imagine that the father would send this reply:

> "My Dear Son: You know that your mother and I love you dearly. Every day we pray for your safe return. Nothing would shock and sadden us more than losing you. But if your duty, if the freedom of our country requires it, we want you not to be afraid. Dying with a good conscience is better than living as a coward. We want you to be faithful to your task, even if it means death."

This is exactly what the scriptural texts are saying about the Father and Jesus. "I am the good shepherd....The Father loves me because I am willing to give up my life" (Jn 10:11,17).

I don't want to turn this chapter into a treatise on New Testament theology. A study of Pauline theology will confirm what we have seen from the Johannine writings. Jesus saved us by his whole life. His rising to life is just as important as his dying; we share in both. Jesus' entire life expressed his self-gift of emptying and obedience. The letter to the Hebrews explains how Jesus is our new high priest. The sacrifice he offered on our behalf was: "Here I am to do your will, O God" (Heb 10:7). The gift of himself, resulting in his death, became the supreme sacrifice of reconciliation that fulfilled and replaced all other sacrifices.

> So God does away with all the old sacrifices and puts the
> sacrifice of Christ in their place. Because Jesus Christ did
> what God wanted him to do, we are all purified from sin
> by the offering that he made of his own body once for all
> (Heb 10:9-10).

It is obvious that, once we have the fundamental picture right,
we may then speak of Jesus' meriting redemption for us, of "paying the price with his blood," and so on. But such expressions are
only valid if they presuppose the biblical teaching that Jesus
saved us through his whole life and that his death was the
culmination of his gift of self. God is not a Melek!

God of Mercy and Compassion

There is good reason for us to remind ourselves of the fact.
Church history provides many sorry episodes which demonstrate
cruelty and hardness among Christian leaders. There have been
times when thousands of so-called witches were burned at the
stake—among them children of eight or nine! These killings were
condoned by priests, theologians, bishops, even some popes. We
know now it was all a terrible mistake, that practically all these
people died innocently; and that, in any case, the penalty inflicted
on them was barbarous. How could such a thing happen among
Jesus' own followers? I am convinced that one factor is a misguided concept of God. The blindness of heart and lack of mercy derive
ultimately from the subconscious conviction that God has such
a hard streak himself. Is he not the God who could even send his
own Son to die on the cross? they would think. He may be a God
of love on the surface, but underneath and in reality he is a hard
God, a God who demands full payment, a God who wants to see
blood! Without knowing it, they were worshipping Melek!

When we read the Old Testament with such dimensions in
mind, it becomes extremely relevant. Our concept of God is so
basic to our whole life, our faith, our service, our religious commitment, that we always need to purify and perfect it. Our concept of God will also determine the sickness or health of our
Christian togetherness as a community. Even a simple — or seem-
ingly simple — story like the one of Abraham's sacrifice opens
up far-reaching perspectives.

"Take your son," God said, "your only son, Isaac, whom

> you love so much, and go to the land of Moriah. There on
> a mountain that I will show you, offer him as a sacrifice
> to me" (Gn 22:2).

For me here the dream takes over again. I feel in myself
Abraham's tension as he goes on his way to execute the command.
He is prepared to do whatever God wants him to do—as I would
like to be prepared. But he wrestles with the contradiction of a
loving God, who himself promised a numerous offspring through
Isaac, making this impossible demand—as I fear deep down in
me that God might be like Melek, demanding a price. And then
the resolution. God is not a Melek. "Don't hurt the boy!" However
God does appreciate the willingness to give what he will never
demand: "You have not kept back your only son from me" (Gn
22:12). What seemed a contradiction, loving his son and loving
God at the same time, proves not to be contradictory at all. What
a healing in Abraham's love; what a healing it can be for me,
for my love.

When Abraham was preparing to offer Isaac, he was confused.
But whatever he did was out of love. Perhaps—putting it in a very
human way—God, too, was "confused" when his Son had to face
death. But he was prepared to let it go through because he could
make it the greatest gift of love.

> If God is for us, who can be against us? Certainly not God,
> who did not even keep back his own Son, but offered him
> for us all! He gave us his Son — will he not also freely give
> us all things? (Rom 8:31-32).

This is not a cruel God demanding satisfaction. It is a loving
Father who revealed to us, through the love of his Son, that he
is pure love. "God is light, and there is no darkness at all in him"
(1 Jn 1:5).

2

Finding the Culprit for Famine and Plague

Lightning strikes many places every year. Sometimes people are killed, sometimes not. A story has grown around one such event that happened years ago. On Sunday afternoon, October 21, 1638, lightning struck the church in a small village in England. Sunday service was going on. The church tower was hit, causing one heavy pinnacle to fall through the roof of the church onto the congregation below. Moreover, a fiery ball passed right through the nave. Four people were killed on the spot and others died later from their injuries. All this happened while people were reciting a psalm.

Lightning striking a congregation gathered in prayer! What could that mean? Who could be responsible for this? Superstition soon found an answer. The landlady of a tavern about five miles from the church remembered that a horseman had called in for a drink that same afternoon. He was a stranger. When he poured the ale down his throat it sizzled, she said. That horseman, people concluded, must have been Satan on his way to the village! Arriving at the church he flew up with his horse, tied the horse to one of the pinnacles of the tower and went into the church to fetch a soul—a man who was sleeping during the service. He dragged the man's soul to the top of the tower. But when he untied his horse, he overthrew the pinnacle which consequently fell on top of the church roof and through the roof onto the people. Then Satan departed with lightning and thunder. The real culprit, therefore, was Satan!

What about God in all this? God, the people concluded, had been extremely merciful, for many more people could have been killed. Richard Hill, who was the village schoolmaster at the time and who was in the church when it all happened, expressed his feelings in a poem which was put on wooden boards at the back of the church. In this poem he thanks God:

> In token of our thanks to God these tablets are erected
> who in dreadful thunderstorm, our persons here protected....
> The greatest admiration was that most men should be free
> among so many dangers here which we did hear and see.
> The church within so filled was with timber, stones and fire,
> that scarce a vacant place was seen in church or in the choir.
> The wit of man could not cast down so much from off the
>   steeple,
> from off the church's roof, and not destroy much of the
>   people:
> but He who rules both air and fire, and other forces all,
> hath us preserved, blesse'd be His name, in that most
>   dreadful fall.
> If ever people had a cause to serve the Lord and pray,
> for judgement and deliverance, then surely we are they!

In other words, God saw to it that only a few people were hurt. The others he protected in a special way.

This story exemplifies what often happens when some accident or disaster befalls people. They look for supernatural causes. At times they will blame Satan; at other times, God. Or they will give God credit for having done his best to reduce the effects of the catastrophe. This attitude, they believe, shows an awareness of God's providence, for nothing takes place without his personal involvement. Some extend this way of looking at things even to their day-to-day experiences. "I'm just in time for the bus, thank you, God!" "I dropped my beautiful vase and it fell into a thousand pieces. It must be the devil obstructing me! Or could it be God giving me a warning?"

Although such thinking and such talk may look religious, it is, in fact, superstition. When lightning struck the village church there was no reason at all to ascribe it to Satan. Nor do we need to see any special intervention by God. Lightning struck that church for physical reasons—as it strikes other places all the time. The accident was a religious experience only in the sense that it gave people the opportunity to reflect on their vulnerability as human beings. Let's see what scripture has to say about this superstition of ascribing ordinary events to supernatural causes.

Corpses in Front of the Sanctuary

In olden times the Israelites were firmly convinced that every disaster should be explained, somehow or other, as a punishment for a specific crime. We read, for instance, that a famine occurred during David's reign. A divine oracle was consulted, which stated: "Saul and his family are guilty of murder; he put the people of Gibeon to death." David made further enquiries and found that Saul, some 10 years previously, had put some Gibeonites to death. David then approached the Gibeonites and asked them what they wanted him to do.

> "Hand over seven of his male descendants, and we will hang them before the LORD at Gibeah, the hometown of Saul, the LORD's chosen king" (2 Sm 21:6).

David agreed. He arrested seven of Saul's sons and handed them over. The Gibeonites hanged them and left their corpses to rot in front of the sanctuary at Gibeah. After a few months the bodies were taken down and buried. "And after that, God answered their prayers for the country" (2 Sm 21:14).

When we read a passage like this, we should be extremely careful in interpreting it. It looks as if it were God who wanted the sin of Saul avenged: "The LORD said, 'Saul and his family are guilty of murder' " (2 Sm 21:1), and finally, "After that, God answered their prayers." But we know from many other examples that it would be a mistake to think thus. What we find in episodes such as these is not straightforward revelation but a record of how the people at the time (in this case around 1000 B.C.) were thinking about God.

God's reaction to such thinking is made clear in other passages. The early Hebrews were convinced that God would punish children for the sins of their parents. "I bring punishment on those who hate me and on their descendants down to the third and fourth generation" (Ex 20:5). In the example of the famine mentioned above, they thought God wanted to punish Saul's children for their father's crime. But God corrected this notion very clearly and specifically. The prophet Ezekiel (580 B.C.) declares at length that people will be punished for their own sins or rewarded for their own virtue. Regarding the sins of parents he does not mince his words:

> "But you ask: 'Why shouldn't the son suffer for his father's sins?' The answer is that the son did what was right and

good. He kept my laws and followed them carefully, and
so he will certainly live. It is the one who sins who will die.
A son is not to suffer because of his father's sins, nor a father
because of the sins of his son. A good man will be rewarded
for doing good, and an evil man will suffer for the evil he
does" (Ez 18:19-20).

The same principle was also laid down as a general rule in the
Law:

"Parents are not to be put to death for crimes committed
by their children, and children are not to be put to death
for crimes committed by their parents; a person is to be put
to death only for a crime he himself has committed" (Dt
24:16).

Who Is to Blame?

This gives us plenty to think about! When the innocent sons
of Saul were put to death because of their father's crime, this was
not what God was asking for. It was what the Israelites *thought*
he wanted. And, don't forget, to this imagined wish of God they
ascribed the famine. They thought: *This famine must be due to
some crime we have committed, for why would God otherwise
punish us? Ah, it must be Saul's injustice towards Gibeon. If we
punish Saul's sons, God will be satisfied and he will take the
punishment away.* We know now that all this thinking was wrong.
The famine was not a punishment on God's part. He was not
happy about the killing of Saul's sons. The only thing we can say
is that God tolerated this kind of thinking until he found the right
moment to correct it once and for all.

We find a similar kind of story in 2 Samuel where an epidemic
is ascribed to David's having taken a census of the people. "I have
committed a terrible sin in doing this! Please, forgive me," David
prays (2 Sm 24:10). But in the narration of the same event in 1
Chronicles, it is Satan who is blamed.

Satan wanted to bring trouble on the people of Israel, so
he made David decide to take a census (1 Chr 21:1).

Again we find the same process of interpretation and ascribing
causes. When an epidemic occurred, the people looked around for
the culprit. It was decided it had to be David's taking the census.
Later, they became convinced that Satan must have had a hand
in it! But taking a census surely was not a sin. In the priestly

account of Israel's journey through the desert, which was written down centuries later, the census of the people is prescribed as a duty.

> [The Lord said to Moses:] "You and Aaron are to take a census of the people of Israel by clans and families. List the names of all the men twenty years old or older who are fit for military service" (Nm 1:2-3).

> The LORD said to Moses and Eleazar son of Aaron, "Take a census by families of the whole community of Israel, of all men twenty years old and older who are fit for military service" (Nm 26:1-2).

Again we come to the same conclusion: In spite of what David's contemporaries thought, the epidemic was not due to a punishment by God for David's taking the census. The "supernatural" interpretation was not correct.

The Truth, Not Accusations

But why didn't God himself point out the mistake of such "supernatural" interpretations? The answer is: He did! That is why the book of Job was written. Here we find a man hit by one disaster after the other. He lost his oxen, his donkeys, his sheep and his camels. His children were killed when the family home collapsed. Sores broke out all over his body. If anyone was a person marked as a target of God's punishment, it was Job! The four friends who argue with Job all maintain that he must have sinned; otherwise, God would not have heaped these misfortunes on him. Eliphaz, for example, states:

> It's because you have sinned so much;
>   it's because of all the evil you do.
> To make your brother repay you the money he owed,
>   you took away his clothes and left him nothing to wear.
> You refused water to those who were tired,
>   and refused to feed those who were hungry.
> You used your power and your position
>   to take over the whole land....
> Now, Job, make peace with God
>   and stop treating him like an enemy;
>   if you do, then he will bless you (Jb 22:5-8,21).

But Job staunchly defends his innocence. Whatever his friends say, he keeps repeating that he has not done anything that would deserve punishment.

I swear by the living Almighty God,
who refuses me justice and makes my life bitter —
as long as God gives me breath,
my lips will never say anything evil,
my tongue will never tell a lie.
I will never say that you men are right;
I will insist on my innocence to my dying day (Jb 27:1-5).

In defending his own position Job slightly overstates his case, but the overall outcome of the discussion puts him in the right. God says to Eliphaz:

"I am angry with you and your two friends, because you did not speak the truth about me, the way my servant Job did....You did not speak the truth about me, as he did" (Jb 42:7-8).

God was angry with them, because their interpretation of the event was wrong. They did not speak the truth about God! Note that the phrase is repeated twice. What God wants is the truth, not the pious platitudes contained in the long speeches of the three friends. These friends imagined they were very spiritual. They looked upon themselves as people voicing God's point of view. But they were wrong. What God wants is the truth.

Let us reflect on the implications regarding our topic. Accidents do happen. Disasters are part of the world we live in. The truth about these happenings is that they will do damage and kill life — simply because nature will run its course. An earthquake may destroy a village. Was God angry with the inhabitants? A drought brings starvation. Is it a sign of God's punishment? A bus driver loses control over his vehicle and some people die in the crash that follows. Did God decide who was to be saved or who not? In all such cases, we are not speaking the truth about God if we look for some special intervention by him. Like any other part of the created world, we too are subject to the forces of nature. As human beings we have to accept our mortality. Our bodies are fragile and will eventually break down, whether by the slow process of wearing out or by some physical accident. Except in some extraordinary case, God will not deliberately change the course of nature to hurt us or save us.

My Ways Are Beyond Your Ways

When Jesus and his disciples walked outside the Temple of

Jerusalem, they saw a man known to have been blind from birth—an interesting topic of discussion for the Jews. For, thinking that a defect of this kind must be a punishment for sin, they did not know to whom to ascribe it. The apostles refer the matter to Jesus:

> "Teacher, whose sin caused him to be born blind? Was it his own or his parents' sin?" Jesus answered, "His blindness has nothing to do with his sins or his parents' sins. He is blind so that God's power might be seen at work in him" (Jn 9:2-3).

The blindness was not due to anyone's sins. Thousands of people are born with defective eyesight or with some other handicap. This is not due to sin. We would be wrong to look for some supernatural explanation. It is due to a mishap of nature. Yet the blindness of the man sitting outside the Temple served a purpose: "So that God's power might be seen at work in him."

And here we have to go back to the book of Job. Job was right in maintaining that God was not punishing him for his sins. But he did make another mistake. Forgetting that he was just a mortal being, he challenged God to explain *why* all these misfortunes had befallen him. Job had no right to question God's actions as he did:

> "I am not afraid.
> I am going to talk
>   because I know my own heart.
> I am tired of living.
>   Listen to my bitter complaint....
>   Tell me! What is the charge against me?
> Is is right for you to be so cruel?...
>
> Why, God, did you let me be born?
>   I should have died before anyone saw me....
> Isn't my life almost over? Leave me alone!
> Let me enjoy the time I have left" (Jb 9:35—10:3, 10:18-20).

That is not the way a creature should speak to his Creator! We have to accept life from his hand with all the limitations that are part of our nature. He need not justify himself before us. In his overall wisdom and goodness he knows what he is doing. Rightly, therefore, God reprimands Job.

> Who are you to question my wisdom
>   with your ignorant, empty words? (Jb 38:2).

God will answer us the same way if we ask *Why did God make us so vulnerable to accidents and suffering?* We should realize that we are speaking about the whole of creation, about the mystery of our existing at all, and of our sharing life to a limited degree. With Job we should humbly confess:

> I talked about things I did not understand,
> about marvels too great for me to know (Jb 42:3).

Humbly acknowledging the mystery of our wonderful but fragile existence is a longshot from attributing specific happenings to interventions by God. The true mystery behind the lightning striking that particular village in 1638 is not why it happened in that spot and at that time; it lies in our world having lightning at all.

> Can you shout orders to the clouds
> and make them drench you with rain?
> And if you command the lightning to flash,
> will it come to you and say "At your service"? (Jb 38:34-35).

3

Give and Take
in a Pact of Love

When we read the Old Testament and reflect on its beliefs, it becomes clear that its authors were wrestling with the concept of God. What kind of person is he? What does he consider important? How can we please him and obtain his blessings? What are the things he considers priorities? It is interesting to observe that from the beginning we find opposing, even contradictary opinions, about God's true nature.

In one such concept God was seen first and foremost as the source and origin of all holiness. God is totally different from us. His world is far removed from ours. God is at the center of everything that is sacred and divine, whereas we are part of this ordinary and profane universe. In order to approach God and be acceptable to him, we must somehow or other penetrate into his realm of holiness. Since the ordinary realities of our daily life are so removed from that sacred reality, our only hope lies in making use of those objects, times, places and persons which in one way or another partake of God's holiness.

We are not far wrong if we explicate this concept through the following parable:

> Once upon a time there was a king who ruled in great splendor and majesty. He was of impeccable royal descent. He always dressed in the finest linen and damask. The food he ate was the choicest and purest obtainable. His furniture was entirely of silver and gold. The king had a high regard for cleanliness and good order. No one could be his courtier who did not have these same qualities to a high degree. One day the king extended his rule to a people who were living in squalor, in huts and slums. The king consented to look after them on condition that they, too, would order their

lives according to his principles of cleanliness and discipline. On certain occasions he would come to visit them. For this purpose a palace was constructed. A few chosen individuals from the people were allowed to approach the king there, after they had been meticulously cleaned. Only the members of a particular family, who had washed themselves and wore the prescribed clothes, could see the king on such occasions. The ordinary subjects had to keep at a distance. They were given their own rules of cleanliness and good order. The king refused to give privileges or favors to those who showed any irregularity in their lives. Happiness for everyone depended on conforming as much as possible to the cleanliness and good order manifested in the life of the king himself.

The Primacy of Purity

Such a sketch of God's place among his people may seem exaggerated. But listen to the following text from Ezekiel. In it, the prophet sketches how the priests in God's temple are to serve his divine majesty. Ritual purity is the highest condition.

> "Those priests belonging to the tribe of Levi who are descended from Zadok...are the ones who are to serve me and come into my presence to offer me the fat and the blood of the sacrifices. They alone will enter my Temple, serve at my altar, and conduct the Temple worship. When they enter the gateway to the inner courtyard of the Temple, they are to put on linen clothing....
>
> "Priests must not drink any wine before going into the inner courtyard....
>
> "The priests are to teach my people the difference between what is holy and what is not, and between what is ritually clean and what is not....
>
> "A priest is not to become ritually unclean by touching a corpse..." (Ez 44:15-16,21,23,25).

More prescriptions are given in the book of Leviticus. A priest must also be physically healthy and without any defect.

> "None of your descendant who has any physical defect may present the food offering to me. This applies for all time to come. No man with any physical defect may make the offering: no one who is blind, lame, disfigured, or deformed; no one with a crippled hand or foot; no one who is a hunch-

back or a dwarf; no one with any eye or skin disease; and no eunuch. No descendant of Aaron the priest who has any physical defects may present the food offering to me" (Lv 21:17-21).

The reason for this commandment is also clearly stated. A person with a handicap would disturb the sacred order of God's temple. "Because he has a physical defect, he shall not come near the sacred curtain or approach the altar. He must not profane these holy things, because I am the LORD and I make them holy" (Lv 21:23). In other words, only those who possess the special prerequisites of ritual purity, belong to priestly family, have no physical defect, wear the prescribed clothes, and have not become ritually unclean by touching a corpse or by any other defiling activity can approach the sacred place of God. For God himself is pure holiness and sacrality. He can only be approached by those who partake to some extent in his cleanliness and order.

The stress on God's holiness and on ritual purity is understandable. We should remember that these laws of the Holiness Code were formulated during the time of exile. They flow from Israel's need to realize the majesty of God and to make up for the negligence in worshipping him shown in previous centuries. They reflect an attempt to bring the people back to God by imposing a system of order and discipline. At the same time, the concepts contained in these laws manifest grave shortcomings. They were bound to present an image of God that would have far-reaching consequences on the way people considered themselves and the world around them. Fortunately, this image is not the original or most prominent concept of God proclaimed in the Old Testament.

Victory Through Impure Rites

It is not difficult to see this when we contrast the previous picture with Elijah's sacrifice on Mount Carmel. It will be remembered how Elijah had challenged the prophets of Baal to an ordeal by fire. First, these prophets had prepared a victim and asked their God to light the sacrificial fire. When they did not succeed, Elijah himself erected an altar in honor of Yahweh, laid firewood on top of the altar and placed a sacrificial victim on it. He then prayed and God responded by sending a bolt of lightning that kindled the sacrifice and consumed it in one mighty flame. It proved a great triumph for the prophet. On that day people turned away from serving Baal and recommitted themselves to Yahweh (1 Kgs 18:1-40). The question is: How would the authors of the Holiness Code have looked on the sacrifice of Elijah? I think it would have caused them great embarrassment.

First of all, the sacrifice was offered on Mount Carmel. According to levitical conviction, sacrifice could only be brought to one place—the Temple at Jerusalem.

> The LORD will choose a single place where he is to be worshiped, and there you must bring to him everything that I have commanded: your sacrifices that are to be burned and your other sacrifices, your tithes and your offerings, and those special gifts that you have promised to the LORD (Dt 12:11).

Further, only priests were allowed to bring the sacrifice. But Elijah was just an ordinary Israelite from the village of Tishbe. He did not wear the prescribed clothes demanded of priests. He was helped by ordinary people, not by Levites as the Law expected. He did not use sacred vessels. He did not follow the procedure described in the Holiness Code. From the point of view of the later lawgivers, Elijah's sacrifice was highly irregular and out of place.

Passionate and Wild

The truth of the matter is that the God presupposed in the Elijah story is a different sort of person. He is a God interested in relationships, in people. He is the god of the field and the forest, of the earthquake and the thunder. He is the unpredictable, passionate and wild lover who has given so much to his people and expects a lot in return. He is the God who speaks personally to Elijah in an intimate encounter, but who can also punish his people by sending a severe three-years' drought. In other words, he is not a God who prizes order and ritual cleanliness as the highest priorities. He is a God who wants to possess people's hearts.

This is wonderfully brought out in the Elijah story itself. In order to make the spectacle more dramatic, Elijah had dug a trench around the altar and had ordered his helpers to pour four jars of water on the offering and the wood. They did this three times so that the whole altar was drenched and even the trench filled with water. When Elijah called out to God in great anguish, hoping that God would not let him down, the response was as wild and unexpected as could be.

> The LORD sent fire down, and it burned the sacrifice, the wood, and the stones, scorched the earth and dried up the water in the trench (1 Kgs 18:38).

This is not the answer of a God who is interested in small ritual prescriptions. It is the mighty deed of someone who gives generously and abundantly. It is a God whose heart is made of fire, the fire of love.

> Remember how the LORD your God led you on this long journey through the desert these past forty years, sending hardships to test you, so that he might know what you intended to do and whether you would obey his commands. He made you go hungry, and then he gave you manna to eat, food that you and your ancestors had never eaten before. He did this to teach you that man must not depend on bread alone to sustain him, but on everything that the LORD says. During these forty years your clothes have not worn out, nor have your feet swollen up. Remember that the LORD your God corrects and punishes you just as a father disciplines his children (Dt 8:2-5).

Notice how everything is translated in terms of personal relationship. The ideal picture of being with God was when he walked with Israel in the desert. He tested them as a father tests and educates his children. He gave them food to eat when they were hungry. He saw to it that they had clothes to wear and that their feet did not get swollen up. It was a relationship of mutual trust, of give and take, of responding to loyalty and affection. It was a covenant in which the personal bond between God and his people stood first and foremost.

Probing God's Mind

The greatest weakness of the holiness concept of God lay in its creating a distance between God and his subjects. Moreover, it enshrined discrimination. Just as animals were carefully distinguished into clean ones that could be eaten, and unclean ones, so people too were divided into those who were clean and those who were unclean. The norms for the distinction were clearly physical and external.

In some way, everyone who was not a priest was unclean and

unholy. Ordinary people who touched the sacred objects in the Temple had to be put to death. Non-Israelites were impure by birth. Ammonnites and Moabites were excluded from belonging to God's people even in the 10th generation. "No uncircumcised foreigner...will enter my Temple, not even a foreigner who lives among the people of Israel" (Ez 44:9). To laypeople, to women, to all non-Jews, God was distant and unapproachable because in their very persons they were profane. Not so for the God of Elijah.

When Elijah was told by God to live outside Israel, he was sustained for some days by ravens which "brought him bread and meat every morning and every evening" (1 Kgs 17:6). It was an unbelievable ritual mistake on God's part! For ravens were unclean creatures. They are very clearly listed among the birds that are not clean: "Every raven after its kind is unclean" (Dt 14:14; Lv 11:15). The food they brought too, the bread and meat, were unclean by their very touch! Moreover, God provided for Elijah in the house of a pagan, namely the widow of Zarephath. This is, indeed, a totally different way of looking at things. Here, not only was Elijah kept alive during the famine, but the widow too was preserved and converted to the true faith. When her son was restored to life by Elijah, she confessed: "Now I know that you are a man of God and that the LORD really speaks through you!" (1 Kgs 17:24). By this confession, she proved to be a better believer than most people in Israel at the time. And all this, even though she was a woman and did not belong to God's people!

It does not need a long discussion to determine which concept of God was accepted as the correct one by Jesus. In his very person Jesus manifested God's will to be close to his people. He broke through all the ancient concepts of sacrality and divine distance. By living among us as a true human being, Jesus once and for all brought us into a direct and immediate contact with his Father.

It is also well-known that Jesus clashed with the scribes and Pharisees precisely on the question of ritual cleanliness. During a discussion on eating food with hands that are ritually unclean Jesus declared a different norm for cleanliness and uncleanliness: Only what comes out of a person makes a person unclean. Jesus thus declared all goods fit to be eaten. What a contrast between the preoccupation with ritual purity displayed by the scribes and Pharisees, and Jesus' concern for faith and love!

Unclean Christians?

The question of cleanliness and uncleanliness again played an important role in the early church when the decision had to be taken that non-Jews also could become members of Jesus' kingdom. It is instructive to read that the vision Peter had before going to the house of Cornelius links the eating of all food with accepting all people as equals. After Peter has been shown "all kinds of animals, reptiles and wild birds," he is commanded: "Get up,...kill and eat!" When he replies, "I have never eaten anything ritually unclean or defiled," he is told, "Do not consider anything unclean that God has declared clean" (Acts 10:12-15). The God of the New Testament does not accept the ancient distinctions of the God of holiness!

Looking at conditions and opinions prevailing in some parts of the church, I cannot help wondering whether there has not been some lapse into the old system of ritual cleanliness and order. How else explain the unbelievable distance created between the laity on the one side, and priests, bishops and religious on the other? Why this stress on all features that would make priests and religious seem different, "more sacred," more unworldly than ordinary people? Why this fear of allowing women to enter the sanctuary or of their taking a greater share in the ministry? Why this excessive stress on a distinctive dress for priests and a mode of living removed from that of the people? Surely, there may be some practical reasons for marking priests and religious so that they can be recognized, but, at the same time, may there not be the unspoken conviction that within God's people there are some who are more privileged, more sacred, more accessible to God by their very status? Could it be that the theology of the priestly charism, imprinted forever at ordination, has deteriorated in ascribing to priests an intrinsically higher status than that accorded to them by the New Testament?

It all depends on what kind of person we imagine God to be, where we think he is first and foremost. If we believe that he is a God to be found in whatever is sacred, more in the church than in village life, more in the liturgy than in everyday events, more at the altar than in the hearts of the people, then we will be inclined to stress physical closeness to this God. If, on the other hand, we believe that God is in the first place a God of relationships, that he is present mostly in the hearts of people and wherever people form a community around his Son, if we worship in him the generous and unexpected giving of his love which is also shown in day-to-day experiences, if we believe that God does not make any distinction between people, then our priorities will lie with the pulse of the human heart. Then we may feel called upon to do quite unexpected things in response to the unpredictable and ever-abounding love that we experience from his hand. We will also be inclined then to value the basic sameness and equal status of priests, religious and ordinary believers. Priests will see their ministry more in terms of uniting God and people than in notions of sacrificial worship and maintaining sacred services. The difference will be one of stress rather than of fundamental disagreement, but the implications will be all-embracing and the consequences far-reaching. A living community of faith, actively responding to a God of generous love, will be quite different from a well-organized congregation worshipping a God of holiness and order.

Discipline of Love

Holiness and order are also required, you will say. No doubt. But holiness and order should come in second place. They should be no more than aids in our service. The overriding motivation for serving God should be our eagerness to give a response to his unprecedented and completely unnecessary act of love. He is a God who made us by giving us whatever we have and whatever we are. What he seeks is not external conformity to rules and prescriptions, but the gift of our heart.

Our response, therefore, can only be one of true love, a love that is not calculating, not seeking security in observing a fixed routine, but anxious to express itself in a life of self-giving and devotion. In reply to God's unlimited love, only total love will do. It will be only natural to love him "with all your heart, with all your soul and with all your strength" (Dt 6:5). In this all-embracing love, we will also find the right attitude toward people around us. Since God loved us so much, how can we refuse to give a similar, uncalculated and generous love to everyone else? Precise rules and prescriptions would be out of place here. What determines our behavior will be a deep conviction that comes from the bottom of our heart, because it has been given to us by God's Spirit himself.

In the final analysis, the difference may lie in whether we accept a magical view of God and the universe, or one of personal bonds. When everything depends on conformity with a sacred order, it is that order and not God which stands in the central place. Our happiness or unhappiness will then be determined by external factors, by whether we succeed in falling in line with the sacred discipline or not. The sacraments will be seen as means to integrate us into that order, or to restore our integration in it if we have disturbed it through some irregularity. Even God, to some extent, is then subject to this order because he has to act through it and according to its rules. Did the Romans not say that even their main god, Jupiter, was subject to fate?

But if we believe in a personal God who strikes a living and individual relationship with us, then God is truly central and everything else instrumental. Sacred Scripture rejects the magical notion and points out the personal concept of God as the correct one. Even Isaiah spoke of this, condemning the Jews for replacing a personal loyalty to God by a set of human rules and traditions. Through him, the Lord says:

> "These people claim to worship me, but their words are meaningless, and their hearts are somewhere else. Their religion is nothing but human rules and traditions, which they have simply memorized" (Is 29:13).

Jesus quotes this to refute the Pharisees' attitude to ritual cleanliness and indicate where the root mistake in that system lay:

> "These people, says God, honor me with their words,
> but their heart is really far away from me" (Mk 7:6).

Jesus came to bring the new covenant in which, according to Jeremiah's prophecy, there would no longer be external laws, but in which God's law would be written on every person's heart.

> "I will be their God, and they will be my people. None of them will have to teach his fellow countrymen to know the LORD because all will know me, from the least to the greatest" (Jer 31:33-34).

It is the option of a religion of sacred order or a religion of the heart.

4

Refusing Pork—
and Make-believe

Not so long ago, in a fraternal sharing among priests, the question of truth and honesty arose. It was generally agreed that in the church there is far too much hypocrisy and false diplomacy. But when we tried to define correct and practical principles in matters of truth, opinions varied greatly.

There were those who maintained that truth should be pursued at all costs. They pointed to the example of Gandhi. In his autobiography Gandhi is sincere to the point of even revealing unfavorable details about himself that he could easily have passed over in silence. He often proclaimed that truth and honesty were absolute values for him. Truth was the last and most important norm of everything. In fact, he stated bluntly: "For me, Truth is God and God is Truth."

On the other hand, quite a few participants pointed out that being truthful may hurt people and do more damage than good. They pleaded for a wise diplomacy which would try to do justice to the needs of people. A number of interesting cases were brought forward which, I believe, illustrate the problem in question. I will report them here as they were presented by different priests.

I am a member of the financial board of our diocese. Lately it has come to our notice that a fund specially established for helping poor children is being used for another purpose, namely, for building a catechist training school. Since the money was given exclusively for the purpose of helping poor children, diverting it in this way is obviously an abuse. Now the delicacy of the matter lies in the fact that the bishop himself made the decision to re-allocate the funds. When we tried to point out that it was a mistake, he reacted angrily. My problem is: Should I keep insisting on the bishop reimbursing the money for the original purpose, or should I let the matter pass so as not to antagonize him? If I am too awkward in this particular matter, I may upset my relationship with him and in that way block my opportunities of serving the diocese better in the future.

In my parish a particular lady whom I shall call Mrs. X wanted to start an association for helping unwed mothers. It was a good idea, but I know that Mrs. X would not be acceptable to quite a few other women in the parish on account of previous frictions. So, tactfully, I suggested that another person, Mrs. Y, should be drawn in so that the two could become official sponsors. I did not want to tell Mrs. X the real reason because it would upset her and perhaps cause her to drop the project, so I had to invent another reason to make my suggestion plausible. I feel that this type of diplomacy is often called for in pastoral work.

Some years ago there was an assistant in my parish who now works elsewhere in the diocese. My parishioners often ask me how he is doing. I know for a fact that he is not doing well. He has come up against the bishop on a number of issues and, to speak frankly, I would not be surprised if one of these days he decides to quit. But when people ask me how he is doing, I give an evasive answer. I don't think it is their right to know the full truth. I believe I have to protect that young priest's good name. In such a case I am convinced it would be a mistake to reveal the full truth.

Nothing But the Truth

Should we tell the truth at all times? Is truth the ultimate and only value? Should everything else be sacrificed for its sake? These are not easy questions to answer, especially because quick answers can easily condone hypocrisy and unjustified diplomatic behavior. I decided to search scripture for an answer. What I came up with was quite startling: I found out that God himself did not always tell the truth!

This may seem a bold assertion. Yet a study of the Old Testament reveals that God allowed lots of half-truths and mistaken notions to exist for a long time. Take, for example, the question of vengeance. The New Testament states quite categorically that vengeance should be left to God, that it is unworthy of a person who believes in God.

"You have heard that it was said: 'An eye for an eye, and a tooth for a tooth.' But now I tell you: do not take revenge on someone who wrongs you. If anyone slaps you on the right cheek, let him slap your left cheek too" (Mt 5:38-39).

If someone has done you wrong, do not repay him with a wrong. Try to do what everyone considers to be good. Do everything possible on your part to live in peace with everybody. Never take revenge, my friends, but instead let God's anger do it. For the scripture says, "I will take revenge. I will pay back, says the Lord." Instead, as the scripture says: "If your enemy is hungry, feed him; if he is thirsty, give him a drink; for by doing this you will make him burn with shame." Do not let evil defeat you; instead, conquer evil with good (Rom 12:17-21).

This, therefore, is the truth of the matter; that we should not take revenge. But how to reconcile this truth with the attitude prescribed in the Old Testament against the people of Amalek? Because they had wronged the people of Israel in the past, God enjoins vengeance in the future:

"Remember what the Amalekites did to you as you were coming from Egypt. They had no fear of God, and so they attacked you from the rear when you were tired and exhausted, and killed all who were straggling behind. So then, when the LORD your God has given you the land and made you safe from all your enemies who live around you, be sure to kill all the Amalekites, so that no one will remember them any longer. Do not forget!" (Dt 25:17-19).

This revenge was executed, we read, under King Saul. God told him through Samuel:

"Go and attack the Amalekites and completely destroy everything they have. Don't leave a thing; kill all the men, women, children and babies; the cattle, sheep, camels and donkeys" (1 Sm 15:3).

When King Saul spared Agag, the king of the Amalekites, Samuel himself completed the job: "He cut Agag to pieces in front of the altar in Gilgal" (1 Sm 15:33). Commentators produce extenuating circumstances here: The people of Israel needed to be protected from the evil influences of mixing with pagan nations; the Amalekites deserved punishment; God has the right to give life and to take it. But the fact remains that a cruel massacre is justified as an act of vengeance. When these scripture passages were inspired, people were convinced that God tolerated vengeance and that it was an attitude that could be justified in certain cases, to say the least. In other words, God allowed them to have a very imperfect notion about himself and about the attitude he expects from people.

God's Priorities

It is only gradually that the mistaken attitude toward vengeance was recognized in the Old Testament. For many, many centuries God tolerated Israelite belief in a doctrine that was only partially true. It was only with the coming of Jesus that God's true mind was made known.

Examples of this kind could be multiplied. To me they illustrate that the complete truth was not the most important value for God. He tolerated imperfection in people's beliefs and morals because he was engaged in a process of education. He knew that eventually he would correct their wrong notions. He wanted the fullness of truth to be gradually revealed, not to impose it at a time when the people were not prepared for it. Since truth is such an important element in inspiration, this realization has momentous implications. It shows us where God's priorities lie.

I would say that people were more important to God than absolute truth. When he called them to become his chosen people, he knew that they were simple nomads with primitive morals. He realized that they could not fathom the depths of his revelation and the full extent of his expectations of them. He was content to accept from them a partial faith and a limited moral ideal. He even tolerated that the oracles they spoke in his name manifested only part of his mind. For instance, when the prophet spoke about the condemnation of Amalek, he expressed correctly that God was indignant about the crime committed by Amalek. However, what was stated regarding the duty of ruthless revenge reflected primitive nomadic practice rather than God's intent. The marvel is that God tolerated such imperfect faith and low moral ideal. It shows that God took his people seriously.

There is a perfect parallel to this in the gospels. Jesus, too, did not reveal the full truth about his own person and his mission all at once. In the beginning we find that he purposely speaks in images and parables people can understand. He even forbids those who suspect his divine origin to speak of it to others. This was a deliberate policy. At the Last Supper Jesus says:

"I have used figures of speech to tell you these things. But

the time will come when I will not use figures of speech,
but will speak to you plainly about the Father" (Jn 16:25).

As in the Old Testament, therefore, Jesus tolerates many
misunderstandings and imperfect notions about himself as a
necessary element in his plan of gradual education. Apparently
half-truths did not upset him as long as they gradually led to the
full realization of who he was and what he came to do.

Courtesy and Subtlety

An incident related in the Gospel of St. John is also intriguing.
It concerns Jesus' going up to Jerusalem to take part in the
festival of shelters:

> The time for the Festival of Shelters was near, so Jesus'
> brothers said to him, "Leave this place and go to Judea,
> so that your followers will see the things that you are do-
> ing...."
>
> Jesus said to them, "You go on to the festival. I am not go-
> ing to this festival, because the right time has not come for
> me." He said this and then stayed on in Galilee.
>
> After his brothers had gone to the festival, Jesus also went;
> however, he did not go openly, but secretly (Jn 7:2-10).

Jesus' relatives obviously had mischief in mind. Tempestuous
Galileans as they were, they wanted Jesus to make a show of his
entry into Jerusalem, possibly to stir up trouble for political purposes. Jesus had to disentangle himself from them. He did not
want his mission to get marred by such political ambitions. That
is why he gave them a diplomatic answer. It may be that his
relatives understood Jesus' statement to be a polite refusal, but
the fact remains that he states clearly: "I am not going to this
festival." What Jesus was really saying could be translated in
straightforward language as: "My going up to Jerusalem will be
according to my own norms. You have no right to interfere with
what pertains only to me." In other words, through a diplomatic
reply Jesus was protecting his own integrity.

Studying scripture we may then draw the conclusion that truth,
if we mean by truth stating bluntly the complete and unmitigated
facts, is not treated as the highest priority or the ultimate value.
For the sake of gradually preparing people to accept the fullness
of revelation, God tolerated the teaching of half-truths. Also,
diplomacy may be rightly employed when protecting one's own

integrity. In these cases we see that concern for the welfare of
the person is the reason why bluntness of speech is avoided. The
good of the person ranks higher than blunt speech.

Candor and Veracity

When we define *truth* merely as a bluntness in delivering facts,
we may conclude that truthfulness is not important. But
truthfulness is more basic than that — and very important. Again,
it is useful to listen to the scriptures. In Deuteronomy we read
that the most important duty of a prophet is to be faithful to the
truth (Dt 18:20-22). Jesus himself came to proclaim a message
of truth. His loyalty to honesty and truth was the deepest cause
of the opposition he met from the Pharisees. After telling them
that they were children of the devil, Jesus said:

> "When he [the Devil] tells a lie, he is only doing what is
> natural to him, because he is a liar and the father of all
> lies. But I tell the truth, and that is why you do not believe
> me" (Jn 8:44-45).

Jesus was to die for the truth:

> "I was born and came into the world for this one purpose,
> to speak about the truth. Whoever belongs to the truth
> listens to me" (Jn 18:37).

It is because Jesus proclaimed the truth boldly and fearlessly that
he became a threat to the Jewish leaders.

It is a matter of life and death in our own times to stress again
the need for honesty and truthfulness in the way we proclaim the
gospel. False diplomacy and hypocrisy are counter to the gospel
of truth we serve. How are the people to believe we are ministers
of him who is the Way, the Truth and the Life if they discover
falsehoods and lies in our talk? How will our words about God
be believed if we are clever and if our words are filled with subter-
fuges? How will our message of salvation be credible if in our daily
speech we are seen to be less than truthful and straightforward?

This truthfulness should extend to more than our speech. It
should be part of our very life. Jesus was disgusted with the
Pharisees precisely because they were like whitewashed tombs
"which look fine on the outside but are full of bones and decay-
ing corpses on the inside" (Mt 23:27). He rejected acts of piety
that were just done for outward performance: making a big show

of giving alms; praying on the street corners standing up with outstretched hands; putting on a sad face when fasting. He wanted us to be exactly what we appear to be, to make our words be in harmony with what we are.

If we are truthful, we will not be afraid to admit making mistakes. This may refer to shortcomings or faults of our own, but it may also pertain to faults committed by the church in the past. Official documents usually start with a long history that enumerates all the great things and good decisions taken by the church in the past. What is sadly omitted is a frank acknowledgment of matters that were neglected, decisions that were taken too late, insights which the church learned from outsiders, mistakes that needed to be corrected. Similarly, when we give instruction on matters pertaining to faith or morals, we serve Christ better by honestly admitting faults and shortcomings in the past than by glossing over them in a spirit of misguided diplomacy. The truth will be known anyway. How will people trust us in what we teach now if we do not even have the basic humility and honesty to admit mistakes committed in the past?

People Come First

It is interesting that the reason we should be honest and truthful turns out to be identical with the reason we should use diplomacy in certain cases; that is, the ultimate justification for both is concern for others and protection of our own integrity. Truth stands in service of love. God's revelation of truth is meant to lead us to a living bond with him in love. The truth we reflect on and believe in is meant to enkindle in us the response of love.

This is also the message in that supreme example of honesty and truthfulness found in the Old Testament, the witness of Eleazar. In the persecution of Antiochus, orthodox Jews were forced to renounce their beliefs by sinning against Mosaic law. Eleazar was put under pressure to eat pork. When he steadfastly refused, the torturers suggested—out of consideration for his old age—that he be given some other meat so that he could pretend to have eaten pork. In that way Eleazar could save his life and, they thought, assuage his conscience. But he replied:

> "Such deception is not worthy of a man of my years. Many young people would think that I had denied my faith after I was ninety years old. If I pretended to eat this meat, just

> to live a little longer, it would bring shame and disgrace
> on me and lead many young people astray" (2 Mc 6:24-25).

Eleazar died rather than act untruthfully. But notice that the reason for his truthfulness was first and foremost his concern for others, for people. His worry was that the young might be misled making them think that conformity to pagan practice was all right. The ultimate reason for Eleazar's death was his love of other people. Eating pork or not eating pork was a secondary question.

We know from later salvation history that the prohibition on "unclean" food was only temporary. It ceased when Christ came. It was due to the Jewish concept of the world rather than to a revelation on God's part. God tolerated the distinction between clean and unclean foods; it was not his absolute prescription. Yet Eleazar died for a worthwhile cause because he strengthened his younger co-religionists. He was a martyr of truth who died out of love. Does not this description also fit Jesus?

5

Building a Home
for a Traveling Spirit

Reading the Old Testament we cannot help but be struck by the prominent place given to the Temple building. The Israelites were by no means master builders. They did not normally care very much about grand palaces or mansions. If anyone did, the prophets would soon point it out as a weakness. The only secular building accorded some measure of description in the Old Testament is Solomon's palace. And it merits only 12 verses. But the Temple building was quite a different matter. Its design, its measurements, its furnishings and its overall beauty are described again and again.

The oldest records, surely, are those preserved in 1 Kings. Building the Temple at Jerusalem is considered by the historian as the culmination of God's gifts to Israel. The work started 480 years (12 x 40 years: a perfect number) after the Exodus. It took seven years. No expense or trouble were spared. Cedar wood was imported from the Lebanon. Stones were quarried in the hill country. Skilled artisans were employed on contract from the city of Tyre. Ten thousand laborers were working on the site over the period of seven years with a total back-up force of 150,000 workers in the quarries. The furnishing and finishing were the finest known at the time.

> The whole interior of the Temple was covered with gold, as well as the altar in the most Holy Place.
>
> The walls of the main room and of the inner room were all decorated with carved figures of winged creatures, palm trees, and flowers. Even the floor was covered with gold (1 Kgs 6:22, 29-30).

The dedication ceremonies took seven days. The historian claims that 22,000 head of cattle and 120,000 sheep were sacrificed on the occasion. It is a story replete with superlatives.

God, we would think, should have been very pleased about this. He was — to some extent. He also had his misgivings, if we may express ourselves about him in a human way of speaking. When David proposed the idea of building a temple, the prophet Nathan brought a mixed response from God. David's son would build the Temple, and God appreciated David's good intentions but there is no trace of enthusiasm.

> "From the time I rescued the people of Israel from Egypt until now, I have never lived in a temple; I have traveled around living in a tent. In all my traveling with the people of Israel I never asked any of the leaders that I appointed why they had not built me a temple made of cedar" (2 Sm 7:6-7).

God had been traveling with the people of Israel. He had not minded living in a tent. It is as if he asks: Why this need of a solid structure? I did not ask for it. Will it improve my being with the people?

In this way the Temple began its ambivalent history in Israel. On the one hand, it did express God's majesty and presence in a tangible form. It could inspire people with genuine love and devotion. The Temple was God's holy mountain, the Israelite's true home.

> How I love your Temple, Lord Almighty!
> How I want to be there!
> I long to be in the Lord's Temple.
> With my whole being I sing for joy
>   to the living God (Ps 84:1-2).

On the other hand, the Temple became a problem. Many people put so much trust in its worship that they shifted from true sanctity to being loyal to rites and sacrifices. *If I am only careful to give God the offerings he requires from time to time, I can go on living my own life*, they thought. And so they enriched themselves at the expense of poor people or committed other injustices. Prophet after prophet denounced this attitude. On one occasion Jeremiah took up a prominent position at the Temple gate and spoke ominous words:

> "Stop believing those deceitful words, 'We are safe! This is the LORD's Temple, this is the LORD's Temple, this is the LORD's Temple!'"

"Change the way you are living and stop doing the things
you are doing. Be fair in your treatment of one another. Stop
taking advantage of aliens, orphans, and widows. Stop killing innocent people....

"You do these things I hate, and then you come and stand
in my presence, in my own Temple, and say, 'We are safe!'"
(Jer 7:4-6,10).

They were, in fact, making the Temple a "hiding place for robbers" (Jer 7:11). The Temple became a cover-up, a substitute for
real morality, a false reason for trust. And just as God had allowed the Philistines to raze the sanctuary at Shiloh, so he would
not spare his Temple if it continued to be an obstacle.

"What I did to Shiloh I will do to this Temple of mine, in
which you trust. Here in this place that I gave to your
ancestors and to you, I will do the same thing that I did
to Shiloh!" (Jer 7:14).

In 578 B.C. these words were fulfilled. Nebuchadnezzar entered
Jerusalem and burned the Temple. He stripped it of all gold and
silver ornaments. He broke its bronze pillars into pieces and took
all the vessels and utensils as booty. Only smoldering ruins remained.

Guardians of Stone and Brick

I was thinking about all this when I visited the Gothic cathedral
at Cologne. It is a very beautiful and impressive structure. Its
central nave is 390 feet long. The stained-glass window walls rise
up to an incredible height of 140 feet. At least 20 generations
worked at it before it was completed (1248-1880). Sitting in the
back of the church I allowed the full majesty of this "temple" to
speak to me. I felt in its grandeur and beauty it did convey the
enormous respect previous generations had for God. It made me
pray.

It made me want to join in with that ancient chorus of praise.
I imagined how, in past centuries, this church was filled with people on Sundays and feast days, how the church truly expressed
the faith of the whole community. And this is where my thoughts
started taking a new direction. Formerly, yes. But what about
now? The large majority of people remain outside the church. On
Sundays only a small group, a "remnant," comes to worship in
this cathedral. I saw how easy it would be to judge the situation

in Cologne by this building, and not by whether the Father and Jesus' message and the kingdom are truly alive among the people.

Vatican II has forcibly reminded us of the fact that the church does not consist of buildings and institutions, but of people. Yet, somehow or other, buildings consume most of our attention. They seem to mesmerize us. We do not think of a place as a parish until it has its church building. We imagine that the most important parish activities go on in that building. The parish priest may consider looking after the building and its functions his principal duty. Instead of shepherds of the flock, many have become guardians of buildings. Why are we so fascinated by buildings? Does God want it, or do we want it? "I never asked any of the leaders that I appointed why they had not built me a temple made of cedar."

Could it be that church buildings give us prestige? Surely that is one of the main reasons why Solomon built the Temple. He wanted Jerusalem to equal other cities in fame and splendor. Could it be that we are afraid of tackling the more difficult challenge of the spiritual apostolate? Is our stress on buildings an escape from having to bring God among the people? Does a building give us a false sense of security, as if, once we have a building, things are all right? We need places where we can assemble for liturgical worship, of course. Furthermore, a good church is a visible reminder of God's presence in a community. But do these reasons really warrant the time, money and energy we devote to church buildings?

One thing I know. For the Jews the Temple became an obsession. After its destruction it assumed even greater proportions in their thoughts. Ezekiel comforts the exiled people with a vision of the future Temple. It is an ideal structure, like a dream. He tells of the lifegiving stream that will flow from the Temple. Starting like a small brook, it will become a huge river. Ezekiel obviously is speaking of an idealized, spiritual Temple, but his contemporaries took the dream literally. They needed a visible structure to hang onto, to hope for.

The book of Chronicles, also dating from after the Exile, recounts the building of Solomon's Temple in much greater detail than the original records. A larger share of the planning is attributed to David, possibly because they could not stomach the fact that the Temple was the achievement of a king who lapsed from Yahwism in later life! Also from this period date the descriptions of what the Tent of the Lord's presence had looked like during the desert years. Exact details are given of the framework, the panels, screens, decorations and utensils. Why all this preoccupation during a time when the Temple lay in ruins or had only partly been restored? The answer must be that the Temple had become a psychological and social need for the Israelites. They wanted God to live among them and they thought the external reality, and detail, of the structure was important.

> "Make the interior of the Sacred Tent, the Tent of my presence, out of ten pieces of fine linen woven with blue, purple, and red wool. Embroider them with figures of winged creatures. Make each piece the same size, 14 yards long and 2 yards wide. Sew five of them together in one set, and do the same with the other five. Make loops of blue cloth on the edge of the outside piece in each set. Put fifty loops on the first piece of the first set and fifty loops matching them on the last piece of the second set. Make fifty gold hooks with which to join the two sets into one piece" (Ex 26:1-6).

God is supposed to have dictated in chapter after chapter the material, colors, and how to fasten the loops and how many loops there should be. It had to be executed "exactly as I have commanded you" (Ex 31:11). There is an awareness in all this of the function of detail in liturgical worship — a point for reflection, no doubt. But it also betrays a preoccupation that would end up in the pharisaism of Jesus' day. Is it accidental that the story of the golden calf stands right in the middle of this dream on the sanctuary? The people wanted something visible to represent God. "We do not know what has happened to this man Moses, who led us out of Egypt; so make us a god to lead us" (Ex 32:1). Could the obsession with the Temple belong to the same temptation—to reduce God to what is tangible and visible?

Temples in Christ's Kingdom?

The Temple was rebuilt in a modest form under Zerubbabel (completed in 515 B.C.). Then Herod the Great began a monumental reconstruction in 20 B.C. A major part of the new Temple was ready when Jesus began his public ministry. He loved the Temple. He prayed in it to his Father. He used it for giving instructions on the kingdom. But Jesus knew that neither this building, nor any other building, could ever be the center of that kingdom. The heart of his kingdom could only be a spiritual reality. "The time will come when people will not worship the Father either on this mountain or in Jerusalem" (Jn 4:21). The body of the believers will be the temple of the future. In fact, each believer will be a temple of the Spirit, just as he himself was a true temple. The old Temple as the central place of worship, as the building representing God's presence, had to go.

Jesus replaced it with a worship without Temple. To re-actualize the sacrifice of his covenant, his disciples were to come together, in any suitable place, to celebrate his memory. They were to take bread, give thanks to God, break the bread and share it, saying, "This is my body, which is given for you." Then they were to take the cup and say his words, "This cup is God's new covenant sealed with my blood, which is poured out for you!" (Lk 22:19-20). He would be present among them in the sacrificial signs and in their being together in his name. He would be present in his word, which they would recall and to which they would respond as a community.

The early Christians used *church* for any community of believers that came together in such a fashion. These believers met in people's homes, in public halls, in open spaces outside the town. They did not have buildings specifically for worship. They felt that God was close to them, as he had been with the Hebrews in their desert years. When the veil of the Temple was rent, a new closeness to God had been re-established. For, in Jesus, God himself had set up his tent among them. In him they had all penetrated into the inner sanctuary.

> We have, then, my brothers, complete freedom to go into the Most Holy Place by means of the death of Jesus. He opened for us a new way, a living way, through the curtain—that is, through his own body. We have a great priest in charge of the house of God. So let us come near to God with a sincere heart and a sure faith (Heb 10:19-22).

What mattered in the new covenant was that all were close to God. "None of them will have to teach his fellow countryman to know the LORD, because all will know me, from the least to the greatest" (Jer 31:34). A people without temple buildings, but close to God.

There is food for thought in all this when we think of the priority we accord to church buildings. If we use church buildings at all, they should be understood to be no more than convenient places constructed for practical reasons. To a limited extent they can perform some of the services rendered by the Temple of Jerusalem: They can be reminders of God's presence, symbols of community faith, places set apart for prayer and worship. But their limitation should also be recognized. And, as Jesus' followers, we need to retain the sense of being a liberated people, no longer bound to any building, truly God's family wherever we meet in his name. As true Christians we will have mixed feelings about sacred buildings. We will respect and use them while not allowing them to dominate our faith and practice.

In this, too, we will be close to Jesus. For while he was clear that his kingdom would not be built on external structures, he regretted the future downfall of the Temple. But when he wept over Jerusalem, it was the fate of his people, not of the Temple walls, that moved his heart.

6

Pouring Perfume
on Tired Feet

A Catholic woman I knew in Bombay once had an embarrassing experience during Holy Mass. I will let her tell the story in her own words.

> Many people were going to communion. As I was moving forward in the line, I noticed that Father Fernandez, our parish priest, was sweating a little. He may have been tired. Anyway, when my turn came, I stuck out my tongue as usual. He put the host on, but not properly, so that it fell off... and dropped on my breast. I froze in horror. He picked it up from my breast and put it back on my tongue. But while he did so, he sort of grunted at me and gave me an ugly stare.
>
> I can't tell you how upset I was about it. I knew it hadn't been my fault. I didn't mind so much the dropping of the host itself. I realize that such things can happen, and surely God understands human failings. But what hurt me was the way Father had kind of blamed me for it. Surely he must have known that I was as sorry about the incident as he was. Did he think I had no feelings at all? For many Sundays after that I went to Mass in another church.
>
> Father Fernandez is quite a good priest. I like him really. But why does he always have to be so brusque with women?

I knew the parish priest in question, and I felt she was right. He is a very committed pastor, with a large heart. But his manner of speaking and acting is often stiff and harsh. He obviously feels awkward when dealing with women, and that makes him abrasive and rough. He lacks refinement and tenderness.

What exactly is *tenderness* and how important is it? Strangely enough, for a good description, and for providing material for prayer, the Old Testament is a much better starting point than the New. The Old Testament, for all its violence and cruder sec-

65

tions, offers deep insights into the more delicate aspects of human relationships.

Affectionate Feelings

When a man and a woman fall in love, their lives change. Their mutual attraction and admiration overshadow everything else. It is as if the whole world is filled with new colors. The ecstasy of such early romance, if it develops properly, will mature into a deep mutual sharing, the stable and close affection between husband and wife. There is something extremely beautiful in this. It is one of the heights of human relationship. It cannot exist without real tenderness.

In the Song of Songs the woman says of her partner:

"Like an apple tree among the trees of the forest,
   so is my dearest compared to other men.
I love to sit in its shadow
   and its fruit is sweet to my taste....
I am weak from passion.
His left hand is under my head
   and his right hand caresses me" (Sg 2:3,5-6).

And the man says:

"How beautiful you are, my love;
   how your eyes shine with love!" (Sg 1:15).

Tenderness means respecting the delicate feelings of another person. There is tenderness in the way the man and woman address each other. There is tenderness in the way she simply wants to sit in his presence. There is tenderness in his embrace, cradling her head in the fold of his left arm, caressing her skin with his right hand. The touch is soft, the language poetry. Each has a heightened awareness of the other's presence.

Are we not in the realm of sexuality? someone might ask. Yes, we are. Sexuality plays a part in this communication of love between a man and a woman. It means that our bodies too become means of receiving and giving feelings of love. Sex is an important and beautiful component of married love. But tenderness is something that goes beyond sexuality. It affects the way in which we receive and give. Misdirected sexuality can be very selfish and hurtful to the partner. On the other hand, there may be relationships in which the sexual component has been reduced through circumstances, without a loss of tenderness. Tenderness is the quality of sensitivity in love. It is to love what flowers are to a plant.

It is worthwhile to read and savor the Song of Songs. For a human being remains stunted in growth as long as he or she is not capable of giving and receiving such love. Note well — I say we should be *capable* of it. Through the condition of our life it may well be that we will never have an actual partner with whom we can have such a relationship. We may, through a vow of celibacy or virginity, freely decide to abstain from marriage — to be freer to belong to God and serve our neighbor. But we should be the kind of person who can, or could, maintain such a relationship of tender love. Those who are not married, for whatever reason this may be, should at least value married love and appreciate the tenderness it requires. The Song of Songs was not inspired for nothing. It is not a secular book, but God's Word. It shows that God delights in the tender love a husband and wife feel for each other.

The Language of the Heart

In fact, God likes it so much that he made this kind of love an example of his own feelings for his chosen people. It is in this context that we should read what the prophet Hosea has to say. It makes remarkable reading. The prophet's own experiences of love are used to illustrate the relationship between God and his people. If we piece the evidence together, this is what happened. One day Hosea saw an attractive girl called Gomer. He fell in love with her. However, when he inquired about her family and her past, things did not look promising. Diblaim, her father, had made her undergo an initiation rite in a fertility festival in honor of Baal. What was worse, he had given her for prostitution to a number of men. Hosea considered all this and talked it over with Gomer. He felt he loved her in spite of her past. He "bought" her from her father for 15 pieces of silver and seven bushels of barley. Then he married her.

In the first few months everything went well. They loved one another deeply and shared their intimate thoughts and feelings. Then Gomer fell back into her past habits. She kept up relationships with some of her former lovers, perhaps to obtain extra clothes or ornaments. She also continued to take part in some of the midnight festivals for Baal. Hosea was sad and upset about it, but he still loved her. He could not bring himself to reject her altogether or have her stoned for adultery. While this experience was affecting him personally, it suddenly dawned on him that his unreasonable and illogical love for Gomer was precisely like God's love for his people. And, in prophetic inspiration, he understood that God was making use of his own experience to make Israel reflect and return to Yahweh. It was the start of Hosea's prophetic involvement.

> When the LORD first spoke to Israel through Hosea, he said to Hosea, "Go and get married; your wife will be unfaithful, and your children will be just like her. In the same way my people have left me and become unfaithful"(Hos 1:2).

Hosea used every means of kindness and persuasion to bring Gomer back. God, he knew, was trying to do the same with Israel.

> "My children, plead with your mother....Plead with her to stop her adultery and prostitution....I am going to take her into the desert again; there I will win her back with words of love. I will give back to her the vineyards she had and will make Trouble Valley a door of hope. She will respond to me there as she did when she was young, when she came from Egypt. Then, once again she will call me her husband" (Hos 2:2,14-16).

Observe the tenderness of Hosea's approach. Even when he threatens punishment, he is speaking to her heart. He wants to create a situation in which he can win her back with words of love. This is the way God works: He is a loving God.

Hosea could be called the prophet of God's tenderness. God is not only a faithful husband—he is also a tenderly loving father. God loved Israel so much that he almost became its nurse.

> "When Israel was a child I loved him
>   and called him out of Egypt as my son.
> But the more I called to him,
>   the more he turned away from me....
> Yet I was the one who taught Israel to walk.
> I took my people up in my arms,
>   but they did not acknowledge that I took care of them.
> I drew them to me with affection and love.
> I picked them up and held them to my cheek;
> I bent down to them and fed them" (Hos 11:1-4).

Who could have described better the tenderness with which a big man handles his tiny son! Tenderness goes very well with strength.

Rather Love Than Zeal

Yet, there are people who think differently. Or at least, they behave as if they think so. The essence of religion lies in keeping the commandments, they say. Faithfulness to God and the service of people is shown in deeds, not in words or in other niceties. "Cut out the softness! Why all this wishy-washy diplomacy and trying to be nice? What God expects is for us to do his will. The person who practices religion does what is right. The smile, the handshake, the exchange of pleasantries are extras. Love God and your neighbor by doing your duty! That is what matters."

Does it, I wonder? Jesus certainly did not think so. He gave a lot of time to tax collectors and sinners. He stayed at their homes and ate with them. The law-abiding scribes objected, "Why does your teacher eat with such people?" And when the disciples were picking grains of corn while walking through the fields on a Sabbath the scribes exclaimed, "Look, it is against our Law for your disciples to do this on the Sabbath!" In both cases Jesus referred to Hosea 6:6.

"Go and find out what is meant by the scripture that says: 'It is kindness that I want, not animal sacrifices' " (Mt 9:13).

"The scripture says, 'It is kindness that I want, not animal sacrifices.' If you really knew what this means, you would not condemn people who are not guilty" (Mt 12:7).

I must confess that the way Jesus interprets Hosea 6:6 is revealing to me. The very quotation itself shows that Hosea's teaching had made an impression on Jesus. He understood that the prophet is speaking about inner attitudes—that these are of greater value than external religious practice. With their stress on faithfulness to the Law, the scribes had lost sight of love. When they met so-called sinful people all they could think of is how not to be soiled by contact with them. They did not see that kindness and consideration rank much higher in God's scale of values. When they saw someone "transgressing the Law," as when Jesus' disciples picked ears of corn, they judged by the norms found in judicial schools; they did not respect the motivation and feeling of the persons involved. "It is kindness that I want, not sacrifice," thus expresses a principle. Respecting people's feelings scores higher with him than being legally or ritually correct. God values kindness and tenderness.

When Jesus went to the house of Simon the Pharisee, a prostitute came into the dining hall. She took up her position behind Jesus, at his feet. Then she knelt down and wept. Her tears fell on Jesus' feet; she dried them with her hair. Then she kissed them and poured ointment on them. Jesus allowed her to do this. He did not pull his feet back and look indignant as the Pharisees would have done. No, he gracefully accepted the expression of love she gave to him. When Simon criticized Jesus in his own mind, Jesus told him the parable of the two creditors and ended up saying:

> "Do you see this woman? I came into your home, and you gave me no water for my feet, but she has washed my feet with her tears and dried them with her hair. You did not welcome me with a kiss, but she has not stopped kissing my feet since I came. You provided no olive oil for my head, but she has covered my feet with perfume" (Lk 7:44-46).

Simon, we should note, had not fallen short in his duties as a host. A host did not need to kiss his guest or to provide water and oil. What Jesus contrasts is the approach, the attitude to him, shown by both persons. Simon might have been correct according to the letter of the law but he had not shown kindness and love. The "sinful" woman, however, was a person who was capable of real love. That is why Jesus went on to say:

> "I tell you, then, the great love she has shown proves that her many sins have been forgiven. But whoever has been forgiven little shows only a little love" (Lk 7:47).

Jesus, in my opinion, was not only referring to the love she had shown to him after entering the hall. No, she was the kind of person who could love. It was this capacity to love that she had now also shown to Jesus in her search for forgiveness. On account of this love he found it easy to forgive her sins. What a beautiful consolation to give to the woman! It was the nicest thing Jesus could have said. It was his tender way of accepting her repentance and giving her new self-respect. "Your faith has saved you; go in peace" (Lk 7:50).

In the rock opera *Jesus Christ Superstar* it is assumed that Jesus and Mary Magdalene had fallen in love. At first I was scandalized by the idea. Later I began to realize that it contains a grain of truth. Jesus was a loving and lovable person. He would have made an ideal husband. In his dealing with persons like Mary Magdalene he shows a tenderness that borders on being in love. What is overlooked in the musical is that Jesus did not restrict this love to one or other person and that he did not bind himself to anyone exclusively in marriage. But he was not hard and awkward toward women. He loved them and showed them kindness and tenderness. Lord, save your church from priests who dislike women and from nuns who cannot show affection!

7

Fixing Our Gaze
Beyond the Known Horizon

Not so long ago I had an argument with a born-again Christian. He had been educated a Catholic, lapsed while pursuing a successful career, then found Christ again in a charismatic second conversion. When I talked to him of the exciting new discoveries of science, he reacted with impatience and irritation.

"What? How can you waste your time on those things! As a priest of God you should be interested in what pertains to God's Kingdom! God has given us the fullness of revelation in Jesus Christ. That is all we need to know for salvation. Everything else belongs to this world and distracts from our main objective. As a priest you should focus all your attention on the New Testament and on preaching Christ. Everything else is unnecessary and a waste. It is of the devil!"

When I probed a little further, I found that he cherished the conviction that Christians know everything that is to be known, and that there is no further need for searching or questioning about God or the universe in which we live.

The incident reminded me vividly of another one of an entirely different nature. On that occasion I was talking to a scientist who did not profess allegiance to any particular church. Yet I found that she was deeply involved in basic religious questions. She believed in God, she said, and devoted some time to prayer every day. She was very much interested in the ultimate purpose of the universe. She considered life a continuous, exciting search with new discoveries disclosing aspects of our existence day after day.

"One of the reasons why I cannot become a Christian, I feel, is that enclosing myself within such a rigid, boxed-in mentality would kill me spiritually. The Christians I know are unimaginative people who seem to think they know the answers to everything. Their doctrine is plainly boring. I could not possibly tie myself down and deny the inquisitiveness of my mind and the wider longings of my heart."

Comparing the two approaches I have been wondering whether we could find some guidance in scripture as to the right attitude. Is it true that all questions have been answered for good? Is Christianity a closed set of doctrines? Is it true that being a Christian means closing our minds to further searching and questioning? Does accepting Jesus force us to the boring and predictable existence implied by the practice and beliefs of certain Christians?

The first, overall impression which Sacred Scripture gives us, both in the Old and New Testaments, is that the people held out as examples to us were living personalities, not automatons captured in a closed system. They were outward-looking people, not inward-looking. The "we-know-everything" Christian clings to a doctrine summed up in a catechism, to a liturgical worship with fixed rules, to ethical practices along well established lines, to the framework of a highly organized community. No scriptural hero defends such values, nor is this kind of faith ever held out to us as a model in the Old or the New Testament. On the contrary, faith is always an exciting journey, a moving into unknown territory with unsuspected adventures ahead.

Inspired Curiosity

Among the many Old Testament characters worthy of study in this regard, the Queen of Sheba merits special attention. She had come to Jerusalem "to test Solomon with difficult questions." After speaking to him, she was full of wonder and praise.

> "What I heard in my own country about you and your wisdom is true! But I couldn't believe it until I had come and seen it all for myself. But I didn't hear even half of it; your wisdom and wealth are much greater than what I was told" (1 Kgs 10:6-7).

What kind of questions did she ask? Perhaps we have an indication in Proverbs where we find reported the words of another non-Jew, Agur son of Jakeh:

> "I have never learned any wisdom,
> and I know nothing at all about God.
> Who has ever mastered heavenly knowledge?
> Who has ever caught the wind in his hand?
> Or wrapped up water in a piece of cloth?
> Or fixed the boundaries of the earth?
> Who is he, if you know? Who is his son?" (Prv 30:3-4).

The Queen of Sheba's questions must have been fundamental ones like those of Agur.

The interesting thing is that the Queen of Sheba is held out to us an an example by Jesus himself. The Pharisees and scribes in Jesus' time were certainly well-grounded in basic religious teaching. Yet the Queen of Sheba was better than they were; she was the kind of person who seeks God, while they imagined themselves to have the fullness of truth already.

> "On the Judgment Day the Queen of Sheba will stand up and accuse you, because she traveled all the way from her country to listen to King Solomon's wise teaching; and I assure you that there is something here greater than Solomon!" (Mt 12:42).

It is as if Jesus says: Knowing a few more truths is not what matters. What is important is the disposition to learn, to seek God, to be open to new discoveries and new revelations. The Queen of Sheba is, therefore, a model of a true believer because she was very anxious to find out about the truth.

Probing Nature

But the Queen of Sheba's interest did not go out only to religious questions. She must have wanted to benefit also from Solomon's newly established secular science. Of course, in Solomon's days, as in our own, secular science and religion could not be easily kept apart. But there is no doubt about the fact that Solomon made special efforts to increase knowledge about the world in which he lived. He had begun to catalog and study nature. He observed things no one had seen before. This was recognized as a special new form of wisdom, granted to him as a gift by God.

> God gave Solomon unusual wisdom and insight, and knowledge too great to be measured. Solomon was wiser than the wise men of the East or the wise men of Egypt....He composed three thousand proverbs and more than a thou-

sand songs. He spoke of trees and plants, from the Lebanon cedars to the hyssop that grows on walls; he talked about animals, birds, reptiles, and fish. Kings all over the world heard of his wisdom and sent people to listen to him (1 Kgs 4:29-30,32-34).

The Queen of Sheba surely enquired about all these things, mixing such questions with the more fundamental ones of human existence. In fact, if we analyze the questions mentioned in Agur's sayings, we find there, too, the same connection between observing the powers of nature and finding out about God.

It is not difficult to see in all this a close and immediate parallel to the search of modern science. Never before has the advance of scientific knowledge been as terrific as in the past 30 years! We can now look into the universe and observe things that happened five billion years ago, in regions so vastly distant from ours that they baffle the imagination. We have analyzed the component elements of even the subatomic particles, revealing a microscopic world of such delicacy and immense power that we cannot even think of it without being overcome with awe. As never before, we understand some of the more complicated organizations of different forms of life. In all these fields it is exciting just to be a human person, to be allowed to reflect on the implications and marvel at the greatness of creation!

Take for example, the air we breathe. On the molecular level, it is full of continuous vibrations we are not even aware of. Every molecule of air is thrown backward and forward through impact with other molecules about five billion times per second! There are a billion times a billion molecules in a cubic centimeter of air under normal conditions. Their movement and numbers transcend the powers of our imagination! Then think of the origin of the nitrogen and oxygen in the air. Current theories suggest that about fifteen billion years ago these atoms were formed when matter condensed in stars. Through gravitation the matter collapsed into itself forming a furnace which made the star burn. It was those nuclear processes that forged these fundamental atoms. Again, we know that in the early stages of the formation of our earth, there was no atmosphere. In other words, there was no shell of air enveloping the world as it does now. Our atmosphere was created by one-celled organisms who lived in the oceans and who produced oxygen as a by-product in their food cycle. They were the so-called prokaryotic cyano-bacteria who populated the oceans 2.2—1.5 billion years before Christ. Through the oxygen released by these small livings beings, the atmosphere was built up around the crust of the earth so that new forms of life could arise that were based on oxygen.

We all take air for granted, but what new horizons do we discover when, in this way, we speculate more about its nature! Does it not move us deeply when we realize that through the air we may be linked to burning stars that existed fifteen billion years ago? And to these miniature organisms of the ocean that produced the first air? Does it not make us feel one with the whole of nature that surrounds us when we realize that in an ordinary lifetime a person consumes about 10 million cubic feet of oxygen? Is this kind of knowledge not exciting for us, precisely because we too, as Christians, are constantly wanting to find out more about God and his creation?

Theological Overhaul

We should notice that scientific discoveries also affect our religion and our spirituality. Obviously they do not change our basic convictions: the truths revealed to us about God and about salvation in Jesus Christ. But new questions arise which demand further search and new theological reflection. For example, the theory of evolution forced Christian theologians to re-think the teaching of scripture on creation. Many other questions remain to be answered. How were religion and morality born in the dawning of human intelligence, in that period of millions of years during which humanity's intellectual powers developed? Were these generations of hominids also covered by the history of salvation? What exactly is the relation between our body and what we have traditionally referred to as the soul? Since science has shown it to be possible that intelligent life also evolved on planets elsewhere in the universe, how does our economy of salvation relate to theirs? Has the incarnation consequences for them also? These are not questions to be dismissed as irrelevant; they will be of the greatest importance for the credibility and integrity of future Christian faith.

The theologians of the Middle Ages, though some were great saints and scholars in their own time, cannot supply us with the thinking that is required today. St. Thomas Aquinas lived in a small world compared to ours. Like his contemporaries, he believed that creation had taken place four-thousand years before Christ. He was convinced the earth was a flat disk extending not far beyond the Mediterranean domain. He thought each star had its angel to guide it along a path traced on the sky. But even within that small world, Thomas eagerly extended the theology of his day by incorporating insights and findings of Arab scholars and philosophers. He would be the first to demand a fresh look at the whole of our present-day theology in the light of recent scientific discoveries. "The more we seem to know about God, the more we realize we know nothing," he used to say. Finding out what we now know about the universe, he would certainly have seen that slogan verified!

I want to be clear that what I am suggesting is not a cosmetic operation in which the new scientific discoveries are inserted into Christian theology as an afterthought. No, it is my belief that Christian theology should have the courage to examine its whole structure in the face of newly acquired knowledge. Being true to its nature as theology, it will, of course, take its point of departure from the sources of revelation. It will also gratefully acknowledge the contributions made to Christian life and devotion by the theology of previous centuries. But at the same time it should boldly face the challenges offered by our new understanding of the universe and interpret the data of revelation within the context of this greatly expanded worldview. If Christian theology does not have the courage to do this in our age, it will seriously fail in its task.

Growth of Understanding

Here again scripture may be helpful to show us how theology can function. What can be more fundamental to theology than the concept of God? But in scripture we can witness a transformation of that concept according to the people's awareness of their world. In the 10th century before Christ, Israel was a rural culture that lived on cattle breeding and farming. The people experienced the presence of God in rain for their crops and help for their livestock. They still believed in many divine powers, minor divinities that ruled the forces of nature and guided nations. Yahweh was believed to be the most powerful. He had chosen Israel to be his own people.

> "The Most High assigned nations their lands;
> he determined where peoples should live.
> He assigned to each nation a heavenly being,
> but Jacob's descendants he chose for himself" (Dt 32:8-9).

Six-hundred years later Israel's world had completely changed. It had become a state, and it had the administration, business and military apparatus belonging to such a new organization. It had also experienced crushing defeats at the hands of the Babylonian and Assyrian armies. By then social and political developments had begun to overshadow the annual cycle of drought and rain. God too was seen in a new light. He was not first and foremost the God of nature, but the master of history. Yahweh could prove to be the only God, because he alone directed the course of history.

> The LORD, who rules and protects Israel,
> the LORD Almighty, has this to say:
> "I am the first, the last, the only God;
> there is no other God but me.
> Could anyone else have done what I did?
> Who could have predicted all that would happen
> from the very beginning to the end of time?...
> Is there any other God?
> Is there some powerful God I never heard of?" (Is 44:6-8).

Again, two centuries later, the Jewish community at Alexandria was exposed to the influence of Greek culture and philosophy. The ideas of Plato and Aristotle had penetrated into people's thinking. God was now approached not through experience but through reflection and argumentation. Interest shifted away from God as director of history to his nature and inner attributes. We read in the book of Wisdom:

> Anyone who does not know God is simply foolish. Such people look at the good things around them and still fail to see the living God. They have studied the things he made, but they have not recognized the one who made them....People were so delighted with the beauty of these things that they thought they must be gods, but they should have realized that these things have a master and that he is much greater than all of them, for he is the creator of beauty, and he created them (Wis 13:1,3).

From early times Israel had recognized the hand of God in creation; now attention is focused on God as architect, artist and model of all beauty. Since being and motion are hailed as the fundamental realities, God is worshipped as he who has Being and he who is the Prime Mover. He is associated with abstract qualities such as incorruptibility, eternity and immortality. In short, he has become more transcendent and more philosophical.

We need not be surprised that the authors of the books of Wisdom always took Solomon to be their model. They realized that they were seekers of wisdom as he had been. It is through God's wisdom, they saw, that one can understand the universe. It is clear that, far from being satisfied with the knowledge and understanding we have, we should be anxious to learn more and widen our horizons.

When we turn to the New Testament we find in Jesus' teaching the theme of "seeking." Only those who seek will find the kingdom, like the merchant who was looking for fine pearls.

> "Be concerned above everything else with what he requires of you" (Mt 6:33).
>
> "Seek, and you will find" (Mt 7:7).
>
> "Do your best to go in through the narrow door" (Lk 13:24).

In all these cases Jesus is speaking about seeking the kingdom, that is, God's new order or salvation. Jesus commends such religious seeking, seeking that gives priority to spiritual values. And though he is not speaking of a general inquisitiveness of mind, he does mean a true *seeking*. Also, when striving to serve the kingdom, we should always remain seekers. It is only by remaining open to new developments and by being prepared to learn new things that we will find the fullness of God's working in our lives.

In St. Matthew's gospel the theme of seeking is further brought out by incidents narrated by the evangelist. In Chapters 8 and 9 Matthew enumerated the persons who benefitted from Jesus' teaching and healing; namely, those who go out to seek him: the leper, the Roman officer, the paralyzed man who is carried to Jesus by his friends, the Jewish official, the woman with a hemorrhage and the two blind men. Moreover, Matthew begins the gospel with the elaborate story of the wise men who came from the East looking for the newborn king. These obviously represent the seekers from all the nations. It is not the Jewish leaders, but these seekers who will find Jesus! And what they offer will not be traditional Jewish sacrificial gifts, but their own riches: gold, frankincense and myrrh. The disciples too are sent out as seekers. They are to go out to all the nations and seek disciples for the kingdom of God. It is a search that will continue to the end of time. And it is also a search for a more adequate theology, a more meaningful and adapted liturgy, a more effective pastoral approach, an ever deepening spirituality. It is only when we seek that we shall find!

8

Ancient Prophets on My Mountain

Christian faith must constantly grow. It cannot remain static. Either it will slowly wither and die, or it will mature and bear ever more fruit. And as the stem grows higher and the branches heavier, it needs to strike deeper roots. Without deeper roots, there is little hope for survival.

> "Some of the seed fell on rocky ground, where there was little soil. The seeds sprouted, because the soil wasn't deep. Then, when the sun came up, it burned the young plants; and because the roots had not grown deep enough, the plants soon dried up" (Mk 4:5-6).

Perhaps we are under the impression that Jesus himself did not need to undergo this process of deepening. Such an idea would be wrong. It is contradicted by all the indications that we can glean from the gospels, no less than by the explicit statement that Jesus grew in wisdom and grace (Lk 2:52). Being truly human in every sense of the word, Jesus needed to reflect, to incorporate new experiences into his self-concept, to reinforce his ideals and nurture his heart and mind with new images. Jesus was the most vibrant, open, sensitive, keen, inquisitive religious leader that ever lived. If his humanity, as we believe, presented "the exact likeness of God's own being" (Heb 1:3), it reflected also the irrepressible vitality of God. At the same time, being one of us, Jesus needed to learn — "Even though he was God's Son, he learned through his sufferings to be obedient" (Heb 5:8). And the need to suffer was precisely a very upsetting discovery Jesus made.

Distressing Premonitions

Since the gospels recount events in a systematic, rather than a chronological way, it is difficult to trace the exact sequence of incidents that led to that discovery. It is possible that the clash with the scribes and Pharisees started it off. Jesus refused to accept the pharisaic interpretation of the Sabbath rest. He cured people on the Sabbath. When he healed a man who was partly paralyzed, "they were filled with rage and began to discuss among themselves what they could do to Jesus" (Lk 6:11). The Law prescribed the death penalty for transgressing the Sabbath, so it was killing him they had in mind. The awareness of this threat became all the more real for Jesus when news of John the Baptist's death reached him. He withdrew to a lonely place to reflect and pray. There, in the presence of his Father, the inescapable conclusion must have dawned on him: If I continue my ministry in this way, they will certainly put me to death.

> "I tell you that Elijah has already come and people did not recognize him, but treated him just as they pleased. In the same way they will also mistreat the Son of Man" (Mt 17:12).

It is easy to talk about it now, but for Jesus the realization must have come as a shock. The hostility of the scribes hurt him deeply. The prospect of having to face pain and humiliation upset him. And, most of all, the threat of possible failure loomed large. Was there no way out? What direction did the Spirit want him to go? How could he be true to his mission? How could he ensure that the kingdom would be established, whatever might happen to him? Jesus needed to re-examine his entire position, his motives and ideals, his feelings and his thoughts. When, in prayer and inner wrestling, he came to accept his impending death as part of his mission, he was, in fact, deepening his spiritual life. He learned; he grew in wisdom and grace; he became more true to himself.

Trying to enter into Jesus' mind obviously is not easy. We necessarily oversimplify the thoughts and emotions that tossed him backward and forward. Certainly in Nazareth, while preparing for his mission, the possibility of opposition must have been in his mind. But if, for the purpose of our reflection, we simplify matters a little, we may say that the integration of suffering into his thought pattern marked for Jesus an important new step in his interior life. What enabled him to take this step? From what source did he draw the images and concepts that made him see his mission in this new light? The answer is simple and straightforward: from the inspired scriptures. Or, to put it in our terms, from the Old Testament. It is here that our analysis of Jesus' progressive self-understanding becomes immediately relevant to our discussion.

The hymn of the suffering servant of God (Is 52:13—53:12) certainly molded Jesus' thinking. But other Old Testament texts were equally important. The following event is revealing:

> About a week after he had said these things [regarding his future suffering], Jesus took Peter, John, and James with him and went up a hill to pray. While he was praying, his face changed its appearance, and his clothes became dazzling white. Suddenly two men were there talking with him. They were Moses and Elijah, who appeared in heavenly glory and talked with Jesus about the way in which he would soon fulfill God's purpose by dying in Jerusalem (Lk 9:28-31).

What took place on that lonely hill? Why did Moses and Elijah appear?

Models and Allies

Moses and Elijah, we are told by commentators, represented the Law and the Prophets. Jesus was to fulfill both. True. But this kind of commentary missed the psychological aspect of the happening. Jesus went up a high hill to pray. His mind was filled with the shock of his future suffering. The determination to live up to his mission "until death" was taking hold of him, but he needed to clarify his vision and to strengthen his resolve. That is why he went up to pray. And while he prayed, he groped for examples from the inspired past that would help him, that would show him how to respond to the challenge. Moses came to mind, and Elijah.

Jesus recalled how Moses had met God in the burning bush, how he had been sent to bring God's people out of Egypt. He saw, in his mind's eye, how Moses protested: "I am nobody. How can I go...?" (Ex 3:11). He relived Moses' struggles with the Pharaoh, Moses' trouble with the people:

> "Why have you given me the responsibility for all these people? I didn't create them or bring them to birth! Why

should you ask me to act like a nurse and carry them in
my arms like babies all the way to the land you promised
to their ancestors?" (Nm 11:11-12).

He felt Moses' disappointment when the people set up the golden
calf, and his exasperation, anguish, and anger. But after all this,
and through it all, he experienced Moses' elation in being allowed to be so close to the Father. He saw vividly how Moses,
high on a mountain too, experienced God's presence.

"I will make all my splendor pass before you, and in your
presence I will pronounce my sacred name. I am the LORD
and I show compassion and pity on those I choose.... When
the dazzling light of my presence passes by, I will put you
in an opening in the rock and cover you with my hand until I have passed by. Then I will take my hand away, and
you will see my back but not my face" (Ex 33:19-23).

And Jesus knew that it was this closeness to the Father that had
carried Moses through until the end of his mission.

Then Jesus thought of Elijah. How he had to flee from his own
country during the drought. How he confronted the prophets of
Baal on the Carmel. How after his victory over them Elijah had
had to flee once more. He saw him there, lying in the desert under
the shade of a tree, saying to God: "It's too much....Take away
my life; I might as well be dead!" (1 Kgs 19:4). But again he saw
consolation in Elijah's meeting with God. There, in the cave on
God's holy mountain, Elijah experienced God's presence.

Then the LORD passed by and sent a furious wind that split
the hills and shattered the rocks — but the LORD was not
in the wind. The wind stopped blowing, and then there was
an earthquake — but the LORD was not in the earthquake.
After the earthquake there was a fire — but the LORD was
not in the fire. And after the fire there was the soft whisper
of a voice. When Elijah heard it, he covered his face with
his cloak and went out and stood at the entrance of the cave
(1 Kgs 19:11-12).

It was this experience, Jesus knew, that had given Elijah the
strength to continue his mission.

Ecstasy and Resolve

Jesus himself was transported into a trance. "A change came
over Jesus: his face was shining like the sun, and his clothes were

dazzling white" (Mt 17:2). The presence of God enveloped him, as it had done Moses and Elijah before. And Jesus felt the confirmation these two great prophets had felt. He heard the Father say: "This is my own dear Son, with whom I am pleased — listen to him!" (Mt 17:5). The Father thus reaffirmed him as the new Moses and as his messianic servant, and gave Jesus the guidance and inner support he needed. From now on he would resolutely set his face toward Jerusalem to meet the challenge head-on. His encounter with Moses and Elijah helped him to do this.

At this stage, being children of our time, we may ask: Did Moses and Elijah appear to Jesus in a physical form? Maybe they did. It seems equally possible that Jesus had a spiritual encounter with them. His talking with Moses and Elijah may have been a very intense, personal confrontation—so intense that he felt they were almost physically there. Jesus told the three apostles about this experience and in later tradition it was formulated as if the two prophets were present as visible persons. We find a similar development in the temptation stories which were recounted by Jesus in the form of a well-known midrash, then taken up in the gospels as narrated events. Such an interpretation of Jesus' encounter with Moses and Elijah does not minimize the historicity of the transfiguration account. Whether Jesus talked to them in visible form or in a spiritual confrontation, the outcome remains the same: He was comforted and strengthened by what they had experienced. And, like Moses and Elijah before him, Jesus was so filled by the Father's closeness to him that he could now confidently accept his death. Peter gives this confirmation as the substance of the transfiguration experience.

> We were there when he was given honor and glory by God the Father, when the voice came to him from the Supreme Glory, saying, "This is my own dear Son, with whom I am pleased!" (2 Pt 1:16-18).

The Role of the Past

From this one happening in the life of Jesus we can learn many things. We see that he had to grow and to deepen his understanding and commitment. We also find that the scriptures provided him with the inspiration he required. It was by his reliving of Moses' and Elijah's experiences that Jesus prepared himself for the special revelation his Father was to give him. It illustrates that much of Jesus' thinking and many of his spiritual ideals took their starting point from the Old Testament.

That by itself would be reason enough for us to take the Old Testament seriously. But there is more to it. If Jesus found inspiration in the old covenant writings, so can we. The Old Testament can also become a means for us to face the new questions and challenges that we will meet in our own mission. Indeed, Moses and Elijah can be brought to life and made to speak to us today.

Part Two

Making the Most of Reading and Prayer

"What shall I do, Lord,
with this quaint collection
of tribal anecdotes,
prophetic oracles,
psalms and proverbs,
intriguing narratives
—the record of your deeds and words
among a foreign people
so many years ago?"

                              "Search them.
                              You'll find
                              message and meaning,
                              faces and feeling,
                              symbols and signs."

"Feed me, Lord.
Still my hunger....
and fill my basket
for the rest
of the day."

9

Munching Words, Digesting Images

It is surprising how we can take obvious things for granted. I remember living in Nijmegen, Holland, for a number of years and how getting around used to be a problem. I found my way by asking questions. I learned some of the bus routes that passed by the house where I was staying. I got to know one or two short-cuts. But it took me a long time to get something resembling a coherent picture. Then, one fine day a tourist stayed with us. She had a wonderful map of the town. Looking at it was a revelation to me. I traced the roads and streets that I knew and saw un-suspected connections. Suddenly it dawned on me that I had been a fool. I should have bought a map from the start! That would have saved me a lot of blundering about! I could have learned the routes methodically instead of finding out by trial and error.

The same frequently happens to our bible reading. Nobody teaches us how to do it. We simply start reading somewhere and blunder on, wondering where it will lead us. Perhaps we have a fixed time — say 15 minutes — and so we read in that period as much as we can. It might be from halfway through the chapter where we stopped yesterday to halfway through another chapter. After finishing one book in this manner, we embark on the next. Interesting ideas do strike us, of course, but they are soon stifled by our urge to read on and finish a good portion. We do retain some inspiration but much of it is lost as well. Is there a more profitable and methodical way of reading scripture?

There is. And it rests on certain presuppositions. The first is that we should make up our mind not to be in a hurry. I don't mean to say that I am opposed to the fixed time every day. Usually that is a good idea. But, while keeping punctually to our time limit, we should refuse to rush through the reading or worry about how many verses we will complete. What we read we want to read well.

To Hear God Speak

At the outset we say a short personal prayer. We ask God to speak to us in today's reading. We promise that we will try to be responsive. There are a number of standard formulations for this opening prayer, but they won't do. We will have to say something personal to God. It makes all the difference.

We then open the bible. When we start a new book with which we are unfamiliar, we read a short introduction to it. The same applies to sections within a book when we are dealing with complicated texts. The prophets, for example, may need a short commentary to go with them. Neglecting to acquire such information will reduce the chance of our penetrating to the real meaning of of the text. However, such explanatory study should be short and to the point. Reading the actual inspired text is, after all, the purpose of the exercise.

The next thing we should remember is that we should read together what belongs together. All writing can be divided into natural sections, into units of meanings. A psalm is one unit; a prophetic oracle another. The historical books can be divided into shorter narrations, incidents, remarks by the storyteller. In short, we read passages, not sentences.

When we read a particular unit, our attention will first focus on the main idea the author wants to convey. This is sometimes called the *fundamental assertion*. We reflect on what this means for our life. If we formulate it in a way that is truly meaningful to us, we call it the *key message*. Later we may make the analysis unconsciously but in the beginning, while we are schooling ourselves in the method of reading, we may want to do it more explicitly. We ask ourselves two questions: What did the inspired author want to tell us through this passage? How does it apply to me?

Perhaps, I should interrupt here. An example might clarify the procedure better than a description can. 1 Samuel 17:1-54 is one unit. It recounts the famous duel between David and Goliath. The purpose of the story can be inferred from what David says to Goliath:

"You are coming against me with sword, spear, and javelin,
but I come against you in the name of the LORD Almighty,
the God of the Israelite armies, which you have defied. This
very day the LORD will put you in my power; I will defeat
you and cut off your head. And I will give the bodies of the
Philistine soldiers to the birds and animals to eat. Then the
whole world will know that Israel has a God, and everyone
here will see that the LORD does not need swords or spears
to save his people" (1 Sm 17:45-47).

The inspired author indicated his intention in these verses. He
wants to teach that with God's help we can overcome any opposition. How does this apply to me? I can overcome otherwise insur-
mountable obstacles if only I put my trust in him. So far so good.
What next?

To Perceive Images and Scenes

After establishing the main teaching of the story, we should
read it a second time allowing the images to speak to us. As we
read the words again we try to visualize what the author is saying as vividly as possible. We try to see it, as it were, with our
mental eye. It does require some imagination, but the effort will
pay off. One scene which will obviously stand out in our visual
recapitulation is the fearful sight Goliath must have offered.
Scripture presents him as a giant.

He was over nine feet tall and wore bronze armor that
weighed about 125 pounds and a bronze helmet. His legs
were also protected by bronze armor, and he carried a bronze
javelin slung over his shoulder. His spear was as thick as
the bar on a weaver's loom, and its iron head weighed about
fifteen pounds (1 Sm 17:4-7).

Did the author exaggerate? He may have, but that is beside the
point. Or rather, we should notice the exaggeration, and realize
that the author is writing like this on purpose. He wants us to
retain an unforgettable picture of Goliath! So we visualize him
as well as we can: an enormous tower of a man, a walking tank,
the incarnation of evil power and menace. In contrast we also
visualize that simple country boy, David, who is only wearing
a loin cloth.

He took his shepherd's stick and then picked up five smooth
stones from the stream and put them in his bag (1 Sm 17:40).

The images confirm the main message we had already discovered. They also awaken our feelings such as fear and disgust toward Goliath and admiration for David.

We are now ready to take another important step that I call *creative elaboration*. At this stage we shift our attention from the immediate story to the higher truths and values it illustrates. Let us not forget that religion is ultimately about God and the borders of existence. All religious symbols, also the inspired words, are aimed at bringing us into contact with this ultimate reality. The story about David and Goliath was bound to time and place. But elements in the story are timeless and eternal. By creative elaboration we try to catch some of those timeless and eternal aspects.

To See Beyond Boundaries

The reflection will be very personal from now on. What impresses one person will not be so telling to someone else. But I will show one sequence of thought the David-Goliath story could lead us to. I am struck by the armor Goliath is wearing. It is enormous. It looks invincible. It covers and hides him. Suddenly I understand that this was precisely his weakness. The real Goliath inside the armor was extremely vulnerable. Just one stone from David's sling can crack his skull! Yet Goliath put all his trust in his heavy protective mask.

The word *mask* triggers another train of thought. What mask am I wearing?

We all wear masks. We present ourselves to the outside world in a particular way, hiding our true selves. At times we spend a lot of energy on building up that mask. Otherwise, we feel, we will not be secure. It becomes heavier and heavier. But inside we remain very vulnerable. Our true strength should lie in what we really are, our true skills. David, though only protected by a loin cloth, was much stronger. Now all this reflection, if it happens properly, is not reasoned out as logically as I am doing now; it is apprehended, so to say, in a flash. We see the armor, the mask, the image we are building up for ourselves as one reality. The many implications of this reality will rush in from all sides. I may feel moved to hang onto this discovery and work it out as a value for myself.

Creative elaboration might also take a completely different

turn. I might concentrate on fear. There are people who frighten me. I read about some of these people in the newspapers— senseless robbers who attack and mug lonely travellers, drunken drivers who may take my life by causing an accident. There are others I may remember from stories told me in my childhood days. Then again, there may be people in my immediate neighborhood who make me afraid. Why is it that I have this fear?

To Discover the Truth About Myself

It may come to me that one reason may be my lack of self-confidence, or a lack of confidence in God. People may do me harm, true, but why should I fear them? If fear means being prudent, avoiding conflict and danger, it is a good thing. But if it makes me feel small and inadequate, I am giving too much prominence to the Goliaths in my life. I should not run away from them and feel defeated for the rest of my days. Like David, I should stand up and fight. They may not prove as formidable as they look. With God on my side I can be as courageous and victorious as David. Again, this kind of creative elaboration is grasped in a simple insight rather than argued out in a long mental discussion.

These are just examples of the way in which creative elaboration will go. Many of the chapters in this book indicate ways and means of strengthening this elaborative process. The main point is that we should not just pass over the story in a hurry, but sit back, create visual images and allow the story to take us into the realm of eternal and timeless truths. Only then will the biblical reading achieve its full purpose, for we will grasp a truth as we never did before and be attracted to it in our feelings.

At this stage we should respond in prayer. It need not be long, but a personal response is called for. After all, it is almighty God who is speaking to us through these pages, and the truths that we have discovered come from him. So we tell him, simply and honestly, how we hope to live up to the discovery we have made.

To Make God's Word My Own

If the text has been particularly helpful, we may want to memorize just one little phrase to carry with us till the next day. It could be: "You are coming against me with sword, spear and javelin, but I come against you in the name of the LORD Almighty" (1 Sm 17:45); or, "You are just a boy and he has been a soldier all his life!" (1 Sm 17:33); or any other phrase. The memorized phrase will help us retain the impact of the story and will gradually build up our familiarity with the actual text.

But reading scriptures like this is like a meditation, you will say. You are quite right. It is reflective reading. During the first 10 centuries of the church most meditation was done in this way. The rule of St. Benedict, for example, does not prescribe a special time for mental prayer or for meditation. But it does lay down *"lectio divina,"* "divine reading," as a daily practice for the monks. By a prayerful reading of the Sacred Scriptures the monks were actually meditating and building up their spiritual lives.

The prophet Ezekiel recounts a strange vision:

> I saw a hand reaching out toward me, and it was holding a scroll. The hand unrolled the scroll, and I saw that there was writing on both sides — cries of grief were written there, and wails and groans.
>
> God said, "Mortal man, eat this scroll; then go and speak to the people of Israel."
>
> So I opened my mouth, and he gave me the scroll to eat. He said: "Mortal man, eat this scroll that I give you; fill your stomach with it." I ate it and it tasted as sweet as honey (Ez 2:9—3:3).

The prophet was asked to digest the divine message. By filling his stomach with God's words, he could make them his own and preach them to the people.

Reading scripture means much more than getting acquainted with the text. It means absorbing God's words and filling our hearts and minds with them, letting them become part of ourselves. Scrolls made of papyrus don't look appetizing. But this scroll will taste as sweet as honey!

10

Blind Guides
That Swallow Camels

To draw spiritual profit from the Old Testament we should learn to avoid pitfalls. The Pharisees depended on the Old Testament, but too often they missed the point altogether. This can be seen from the way they interpreted Deuteronomy 6:8, part of the so-called *Shemah* text.

> "Israel, remember this! The LORD—and the LORD alone—is our God. Love the LORD your God with all your heart, with all your soul, and with all your strength. Never forget these commands that I am giving you today. Teach them to your children. Repeat them when you are at home and when you are away, when you are resting and when you are working. Tie them on your arms and wear them on your foreheads as a reminder" (Dt 6:4-8).

The meaning of the passage is clear. Israel should love Yahweh above everything else, and the people remember this at any time and in any place. "Tie them on your arms and wear them on your foreheads" means that all work (symbolized by the arms) and all plans (symbolized by the forehead) should be filled with an awareness of the love due to God. But the Pharisees took the verse literally. They prepared small capsules in which they enclosed tiny scraps of parchment with the words of Deuteronomy 6:4-9. They tied one capsule to their forehead, another to their left wrist. This external practice became more important to them than observing what God had really commanded, namely, to rule their whole lives by love.

> "They do everything so that people will see them. Look at the straps with scripture verses on them which they wear on their foreheads and arms, and notice how large they are!" (Mt 23:5).

But should scripture not be taken literally? The answer is yes if by "literally" we mean what the original author had in mind; the answer is no if we mean that we take the words just as they stand, in their superficial, word-for-word sense. The inspired author of Deuteronomy 6:8 did not prescribe that scripture texts be tied to the forehead or wrist. Taking his words literally is missing the point of what he really wanted to say. It goes counter to the true meaning of scripture.

The Search For Meaning

The branch of biblical science that deals with meaning is called *hermeneutics*, that is, the science of interpretation. It is a difficult science. It has a long history because even the earliest Christian writers saw the need of discussing scriptural meaning. Many of the Fathers of the Church wrote on the subject; so did theologians of the Middle Ages, the champions of the Reformation and their opponents, and scholars of our own day. Even though there is agreement on general principles today, differences of opinion, of emphasis, remain. What from all this do we need for our spiritual reading of the Old Testament? Or could we simply ignore it?

We may not. After all, meaning is one of the principal ingredients of communication. If we miss the meaning of scripture, we are no longer listening to God. A text that is wrongly understood is as a plane that has lost its direction, as an envelope without its letter. So, while trying to avoid the more subtle and academic discussion of the matter, we will have to devote some thought to correct and incorrect interpretations.

To be practical and down-to-earth, there are five meanings or senses that we should be able to distinguish:

1) The literal sense (the meaning intended by the sacred author).

2) The fundamentalistic sense (the meaning based on a word-for-word interpretation of the text).

3) The accommodated sense (a meaning imputed to the text on account of free associations of thought).

4) The applied sense (the application of the literal meaning to one's own life).

5) The fuller sense (a more complete meaning of an Old Testament passage in the light of New Testament revelation).

Complicated, you may think. No, it is not so difficult, once we are used to the terms. In this chapter we will contrast the literal and fundamentalistic senses. The next chapter will reflect on the accommodated and applied senses. The one after that will bring the fuller sense into view. But let us first return to the Pharisees.

Deuteronomy 6:8 said, "Tie these words on your arms and wear them on your foreheads as a reminder." By following the letter of this prescription, the Pharisees interpreted it in a fundamentalistic sense. The literal meaning of the text, however, the meaning intended by the sacred author, was that one should never forget to love God. If we give the matter some thought we will see that this literal meaning is much more demanding than the fundamentalistic one. Having little rolls of parchment dangling from one's wrist and forehead does not cost much; loving God at all times does. What is more, the external interpretation of the law can easily function as an escape, making one forget the real obligation! It might even lead to religious show-business, as Jesus was pointing out: Contrary to what one might expect, following the letter of the law did not lead to greater faithfulness, but rather to actions that were just the opposite of what the inspired author meant!

Jesus gives another example. The Law commanded that one-tenth of the harvest be set aside as a gift to God. "Set aside a tithe — a tenth of all that your fields produce each year" (Dt 14:22). The Pharisees took the word "all" in a very fundamentalistic sense. They maintained that even if one grew just a few types of vegetables, one-tenth part of each variety had to be set aside. But while they were concerned about meticulous accuracy in such external details, they missed what the Law was really asking for.

> "You give to God one tenth even of the seasoning herbs, such as mint, dill, and cumin, but you neglect to obey the really important teachings of the Law, such as justice and mercy and honesty. These you should practice, without neglecting the others. Blind guides! You strain a fly out of your drink, but swallow a camel!" (Mt 23:23-24).

What looks like exemplary fidelity to the text turns out to be treason because it misses the real intention of God's Word. A sad state indeed! It warns us to be on our guard. We may not just lift a sentence out of scripture and interpret it on its face value. We have to study the meaning it had for the author.

The Spirit Gives Life, the Letter Kills

At times, the literal sense, the meaning intended by the author, is not so obvious. We may need to study the context of the piece of writing, the literary forms of expression, its connection with what went before or what comes after. It is not the external words that should preoccupy us, their meaning taken from a dictionary, but what the author had in mind. The intention of the author constitutes the literal sense, and it is this which is the only safe basis for all study and reflection of scripture. In his famous encyclical *Divino Afflante Spiritu* Pius XII stated that we should first and foremost discern the literal sense of a text "so that the mind of the author be made clear." Vatican II put it in this way:

> All that the inspired authors, or sacred writers, affirmed should be regarded as affirmed by the Holy Spirit....It follows that the interpreter of the Sacred Scriptures, if he is to ascertain what God has wished to communicate to us, should carefully search out the meaning which the sacred writers really had in mind, that meaning which God had thought well to manifest through the medium of their words (*Divine Revelation*, Nos. 11-12).

It is the literal sense, the sense intended by the human author, which should be the guiding principle for interpretation.

The fundamentalistic sense is wrong because it only rests on the sound of the words, not on what the inspired author wanted to say. For instance, in Genesis 3:16 God says to Eve: "I will increase your trouble in pregnancy and your pain in giving birth." Taken at face value these words seem to teach: (1) God purposely made childbirth more difficult than it needed to be; and (2) this is a punishment for woman's sins. Was this the meaning intended by the author? Certainly not! Genesis 2:4—3:24 is a parable in which the author reflects on humankind's alienation from God. Our sufferings are seen as signs of our loss of friendship with God. The author mentions some striking examples: the sweat and toil required to make the soil produce food, the pain of childbirth. Neither of these two examples are specific punishments, aimed at specific people. God does not punish farmers more than skilled laborers, or women more than men. By generalizing and absolutizing the image of Genesis 3:16 we are distorting its meaning.

Jehovah's Witnesses, as a rule, refuse to have blood transfusions. Occasionally this refusal leads to a death — say after an accident or in a difficult delivery. They justify their refusal with the statement that God has forbidden it. Leviticus 17:1-14 teaches that blood is sacred. "You shall not eat the blood of any creature, for the life of every creature is in its blood; whoever eats it shall be cut off" (Lv 17:14, *RSV*). Thus, they argue, blood transfusion, being a feeding upon blood, is unscriptural and forbidden by God! This fundamentalistic interpretation, however, is absurd. Leviticus 17:1-14 is not speaking of human blood, but of animal blood. It forbids eating blood with the mouth, not receiving it into one's veins in the course of a medical procedure. The reason for the prohibition was the fact that animal blood was used to make atonement (Lv 14:11). Last but not least, the Old Testament writer had absolutely no idea of anything as sophisticated as blood transfusion. Therefore, he could not refer to it in any specific sense. With the ritual laws having been abolished through the New Testament, the message that remains, based on the literal sense, is respect for human life. Such a respect would be an argument in favor of blood transfusions rather than against them.

Christmas trees provide another illustration. These too are prohibited by Jehovah's Witnesses because of a passage in Jeremiah:

"The religion of these people is worthless.
A tree is cut down in the forest;
...and decorated with silver and gold" (Jer 10:3-4).

What to make of this? Again, we need to look carefully at the true meaning of the passage. Jeremiah condemns idol worship. The tree in the text is "carved by the tools of the woodcarver" (v.3) and is called an idol that cannot speak and cannot cause any harm or do any good. The Christmas tree is no more than an innocent decoration that had its origin in ancient winter customs of the European peoples. In no way is it considered by anyone to be an idol. The mention of the words "tree" and "decorated with silver and gold" does not give us the right to link the text to Christmas trees. What matters is Jeremiah's intention — which was to denounce idols, not festive decorations!

What is the reason for fundamentalism? Is it simplicity or stupidity? Perhaps. But sometimes the real cause lies deeper. It takes courage to believe in a God who is a transcendent and spiritual being; to follow the spiritual principles dictated by one's conscience. It is much easier to cling to externals as the supporting framework of one's religion. Fundamentalists are insecure people. They prefer to rely on physical presence in the liturgy, on participation in visible rituals of grace, on the letter of the inspired word rather than on its spirit. For these external things can, somehow, be got hold of and become a guarantee of being all right with God. The fundamentalist approach comes close to making religion a magical practice. For the external realities, whether rites, customs or texts, are considered to have religious power in themselves, which is the essence of magical religion. But we know that however much God may use rites, symbols and human words, these are only means and signs. The true religious realities are the spiritual ones which cannot be seen or controlled by magical acts. Therefore it is the intention, not the external word, the spirit not the letter that count.

Putting God to the Test

A form of fundamentalism I have come across in recent years is the quasi-charismatic "stick-your-knife-into-the-book" approach. What I mean is that some people have begun to use scripture as a source of oracular information. Suppose I have been invited to attend a particular apostolic meeting. I don't know if I should take part. I already have so many commitments....I may be taking on too much....But then again, God may want me to take up this new task. What shall I do? To find out, to have an indication of God's will and God's pleasure, I say a prayer and open a bible at random. The text which my eye meets on the page I have opened will contain a valuable pointer! If my eye falls on, "People who promise things that they never give are like clouds and wind that bring no rain" (Prv 25:14), I realize I should not go because I may take on commitments I will not be able to carry out. But if I find the words, "I was glad when they said to me, Let us go to God's House" (Ps 122:1), I decide God wants me to undertake this new task, and to do it joyfully. Many texts of scripture, of course, are neutral, so I may, at my own convenience, interpret them as I think best, or allow my eye to rove on until it finds a more explicit statement.

If such a practice is looked upon as no more than a joke, or a game like throwing up a coin to force a heads-or-tails decision, no harm is done. But if we actually think such a random reading conveys a message from God in response to a specific query, things are different. We are, then, in fact, attributing a magical property to scripture. Neither are we being very original. This type of bible consultation in which chance words, estranged from their literal sense and original context, are given an oracular function was a superstition practiced in the Middle Ages. It is not to be recommended, not even as a game. God does not speak to us in that way. Rather we should have the courage, after prayer and reflection, to make our own considered decision. It will lack the comfort of the external "pointer," but will be much more reliable, for it will rest on the internal spiritual discernment of our mind and our heart.

Associations and Puns

Talking about playing a game with scripture gives me the opportunity of briefly introducing the accommodated sense. In the next chapter we will discuss it at length. Here I would like to do no more than compare it with the fundamentalistic sense. Both senses have in common that they attribute a meaning to scripture which was not in the mind of the original author. But in the case of the accommodated sense, it is more a matter of free associations of thought, not of claiming a divine sanction. An example may make this clear. At the conclusion of a drama and song competition in a school, the principal may speak the following words in his official address:

> There are far more stars in our school than I had thought. Of course, we should remember what we read in Psalm 147, that God alone has "decided on the number of the stars and calls each one by name." I am now going to call some of you by name, realizing there may be some greater stars among you only known to God.

There is nothing malicious in quoting scripture in this manner. But we should not imagine for a moment that the text is used in a true *scriptural* sense. Psalm 147:4 speaks of the heavenly bodies we can see in the sky at night, not of film stars or other talented persons.

The Fathers of the Church and theologians in the Middle Ages drew many spiritual teachings from scripture which were really more due to their own pious imaginations than to scripture. This spiritual or allegorical sense, as they called it, was nothing else

but a baptized version of the accommodated sense. When St. John
Chrysostom discusses how Jesus could be God and man at the
same time, he quotes Exodus which describes God appearing to
Moses in the burning bush: Moses saw that the bush was on fire
but that it was not burning up (Ex 3:2). Chrysostom says:

> Miraculous! The fire in the bush spoke with a clear voice.
> It said: "I am the God of your father, the God of Abraham."
> Therefore, it was the Lord himself, in the form of fire. He
> filled the whole bush and distended its branches, but he did
> not burn it up....This was a prediction, a clear image of the
> mystery of Christ to come. For just as the bush could tolerate
> the fire, so Christ's human nature could tolerate God's maj-
> esty. Our intellect and our human reason do not allow us
> to see how divinity and humanity could be joined in one
> natural one-ness. But they were united, that is, in Christ.
> —*Easter Homily* 17

The burning bush is indeed an interesting image of the union of
the two natures in Christ. But did the author of Exodus 3:1-6 have
this in mind when he wrote the story? Certainly not. The way
Chrysostom uses the text is, therefore, no more than an accom-
modation. Strictly speaking he could not appeal to it as something
conveyed to us by God. The link with the incarnation was an
association of his own making, not a message covered by inspiration.

It will be clear from the preceding pages that it is the fundamentalists who err most seriously concerning the meaning of scripture. Their interpretation of texts does not spring from a different
grammar or vocabulary; it originates in a mind-set that attributes
exaggerated value to external things at the expense of inner
religiosity. The fundamentalist often appears in the guise of a
religious fanatic. But what he or she is fanatical about is imposing an external structure of beliefs and practices while overlook-
ing the truly spiritual values or rejecting them as inadequate.

This is the danger Jesus speaks of in Matthew 23:1-36. His
speech is a lasting warning to all letter-cavilers, literalists and
legalists; to fanatics, fundamentalists and false reformers; to
word-worshippers, witch-hunters and whitewashed tombs. While
fanatically clinging to the letter of the Law, he tells them,
they "neglect to obey the really important teachings of the Law,
such as justice and mercy and honesty." With unjust accusa-

tions they handed Jesus over to Pilate to see him killed. Yet they refused to enter Pilate's palace because "they wanted to keep themselves ritually clean, in order to be able to eat the Passover meal" (Jn 18:28). God save us from people like that!

11

Welcome to
the King of Glory

Imagine you are a member of your parish's liturgical committee preparing for the dedication of your new parish church. The
local bishop will preside over the function, but your parish
priest has been asked to preach the festive homily. He in turn—
and so you see how democratizing the church does at times lead
to passing the buck!—has asked your committee to furnish the
contents of the sermon. What are you going to have him say?
What scripture text should he take as his point of departure?
Mulling this over in your mind you remember Psalm 24:

> Lift up your heads, O gates!
>   and be lifted up, O ancient doors!
>   that the King of glory may come in.
> Who is the King of glory?
>   The Lord, strong and mighty
>   the Lord, mighty in battle!
> Lift up your heads, O gates!
>   and be lifted up, O ancient doors!
>   that the King of glory may come in.
> Who is this King of glory?
>   The Lord of hosts
>   he is the King of glory! (Ps 24:7-10, *RSV*).

There are obviously many possibilities in this passage. The community that has prepared its new place of worship must now open
wide the gates of its hearts! The town where the church has been
built has quite a long history, which works well with the
"ancient doors" phrase. To receive Jesus in the new church, the
people should enlarge their past religious attitudes: their gates
should lift their heads, their doors grow higher. The person who
will now take his residence among them is none other than Jesus

107

Christ, the lord of glory. He is the mighty because he is equal
to the Father. He is the strong because he won the victory through
his resurrection. The text, you think, would serve well to illustrate
the meaning of the dedication event.

Now all this sounds very promising, but suppose it suddenly
strikes you that the message you are finding in the psalm is more
your own imagination than the message inspired by God. Maybe
you mentioned your train of thought to your parish priest and
he seemed hesitant.

"Joe," he says, "I am afraid the text cannot really be used
for our homily."

"Why not?" you want to know.

"It is not the original meaning of the passage. It is only the
accommodated sense."

"What on earth do you mean by that?" you exclaim.

"The accommodated sense is only an artificial meaning which
we give to a text because of external resemblances. It was not
what the original author had in mind."

"So? But then the text would be useless."

"Yes, it would. When we are using the accommodated sense
we are not teaching what God wants to say."

"How do you know what God wants to say?"

"Through the literal meaning of the text; that is, by finding
out what the original author had in mind."

"OK, granted. But what did the original author have in
mind?"

"Well, this particular psalm is an enthronization song. It's
all about the ark of the covenant being carried into the Temple."

"But if it's about the ark entering the Temple, why can't we
apply it to Christ entering the new church?"

You sound convincing and convinced, but the damage has been
done. A doubt has been sown in your mind. What is the exact
difference between a too liberal use of the text (the accommodated
sense) and a legitimate application of its inspired message (the
applied sense)? It is this practical question we will be consider-
ing in this chapter. How can we be true to God's word and yet
apply it daringly to present-day situations? It is a skill we learn
more from seeing good and bad examples than from absorbing
definitions.

A Spurious Entry

Let us for a moment step back into the world of fancy — which can so often teach us much about reality! Let's say Pete, your parish priest, had some reasons of his own for advising you the way he did. He had come across Psalm 24 before, in a manner he would not easily forget.

It had been Pete's second year in the major seminary. Every day some students came to the seminary by bus in order to follow the lectures. In the beginning they came by public transport, but the municipal service proved to be rather unreliable and the students often arrived late. This led the seminary authorities to buy a secondhand bus. The bus was solemnly driven into the seminary compound late one evening during recreation. With the whole seminary population cheering and looking on, the rector positioned himself behind the steering wheel and started maneuvering the vehicle into the garage. Halfway in it got stuck; the top was firmly jammed against the upper lintel of the doors. It could not go either backward or forward. To avoid further damage, the rector decided to leave the bus in this awkward state until the following day. Both staff and students had a heyday joking and commenting on the incident.

The next morning at lauds, it happened to be Pete's turn to intone the psalms. It was the custom at the time for the prayer leader to insert his own reflections at appropriate places. When Pete saw that Psalm 24 was coming up, he could not resist the temptation of saying: "This psalm seems very apt today.'Lift up your heads; O gates! Be lifted up, O ancient doors! That the King of glory may come in.' Let us pray that our bus may be very useful to the seminary for many years to come."

There had been smiles and sniggers throughout the chapel. That same morning our "hero" received a public dressing-down from the professor of Sacred Scripture.

"To begin with, we don't crack jokes in church! Second, referring to this psalm was completely out of place. The psalm speaks of God entering his Temple as the king of glory. Applying the psalm's words to the bus and to the doors of the garage was wrong because you gave them a totally different meaning. The external words may have fit the situation, but the real meaning of the text is miles away. You used the accommodated sense. It is not a real sense of scripture and should be avoided."

"Many preachers use the accomodated sense," Pete had ventured to say. The reply was a long, drawn-out lecture on the evils of the accommodated sense.

"Whenever you use scripture, whether you preach or teach or give conferences, the lecturer concluded, always stick to the literal sense." The students felt that a sense of humor was equally important, but all the same, the lecture had its effect.

Let us stop here to reflect. Joking apart (and jokes do have their place in life!), applying "Lift up your heads, O gates!" to the garage doors was, indeed, incorrect. One could never claim that the psalm was referring to this situation, even less that God was saying something to us about it through the psalm. This kind of accommodated sense is so far off the mark that its emptiness can easily be recognized. But what about the following example?

This is a fragment from the apocryphal Gospel according to Nicodemus that is undoubtedly based on preaching in the early church. Christ had promised that he would conquer the "gates of hell." The creed states that after his death he "descended into hell." Psalm 24: 7-10 is reconstructed as a description of what happened when Christ entered:

> A voice, powerful as thunder, resounded: "O gates, lift high your heads; grow higher, ancient doors. The king of glory will enter!"
>
> When Hell heard this, he said to Satan: "Go outside and offer as much resistance as you can." Satan complied and went outside. Then Hell said to his assisting demons: "Close the ancient doors, lock them, secure them with iron bars. Draw up in battle formation and be ready. For if he manages to enter, then woe to us, he will defeat us utterly!"
>
> When the ancestors captured in Hell heard this they began to mock and jeer, saying "O you insatiable, devouring glutton. Open up, let him enter the king of glory! O death, where is your victory? O death, where is your sting?"
>
> Again the voice resounded, shouting: "O gates, lift high your heads!" When Hell heard the voice the second time he answered as if he were ignorant, "Who is this king of glory?"
>
> The angels of his Majesty replied: "The Lord, the mighty, the valiant; the Lord, the valiant in war!" And while they were speaking these words, the ancient gates were broken down, the iron bars smashed. All the dead who had been

imprisoned were freed from their chains. And then the King
of Glory entered, like a son of man in appearance and all
the darkness of Hell was bathed in light (Gospel acc. to
Nicodemus 22: 1-3).

Employing Psalm 24 to visualize Christ's "descent into hell"
does make interesting reading. But it is using the text in an accommodated sense. No one could maintain that it is a natural
extension of the original meaning.

Establishing a Solid Base

Talking about this original meaning, let us consider it
somewhat more carefully. What did Psalm 24:7-10 express? It intended to highlight the significance of the moment when the ark
of the covenant was carried into the Temple precinct. God was
believed to be present on top of the ark in a special way. When
the ark entered the gates, God took renewed possession of his
holy place. It reminded the Israelites of God pervading the Taber-
nacle in the desert: "Then the cloud covered the Tent and the
dazzling light of the LORD's presence filled it" (Ex 40:34). It recalled the solemn opening of the Temple under Solomon:

> Then the priests carried the Covenant Box into the
> Temple and put it in the Most Holy Place....As the priests
> were leaving the Temple, it was suddenly filled with a cloud
> shining with the dazzling light of the LORD's presence
> (1 Kgs 8:6,10-11).

It is natural for the church to apply this text to Christ's triumphant entry into heaven at his exaltation. That is why Psalm
24:7-10 is featured on Holy Saturday, during Easter week and
in a Sunday liturgy. "The gates of heaven were opened up to
Christ because he was lifted up in the flesh," St. Irenaeus said.
It was also applied understandably to the incarnation, to Christ
entering the womb of our Lady. It was sung for that reason on
feasts of Mary. In both of these cases we cannot speak of a "fuller
sense" of the kind to be explained in the next chapter because
Psalm 24: 7-10 is not explicitly applied to Christ in the New Testament. But both are examples of a true applied literal sense. Both
are genuine extensions of God entering and occupying his holy
place.

What about using Psalm 24:7-10 at a church dedication? From
the foregoing paragraphs it is clear that this use of the text is

entirely justified. Dedicating a church and establishing in it the sacramental presence of Christ form an exact contemporary equivalent of the ark of the covenant sanctifying the Temple. It is for our own days what the psalm wanted to celebrate: God filling his holy place with his presence. So your intuition was right. Of course, you would have to be careful in your elaboration of the details. By taking these too literally— "the ancient doors," for example — you might imply meanings not intended in the original passage. Or, you might undersell the text.

Making the Text Speak

Granted that Psalm 24:7-10 may legitimately be applied to the consecration of a new church, how does one proceed further? A frequent mistake is to use the text as an ornament, a quotation that merely embellishes what we want to say anyway. To put it crudely: There are certain ideas we already have regarding an event like a church consecration, so that the content of our reflection is fixed from the start. We only turn to scripture for texts that may give it more style. We have already built the house; the scripture quotations are paintings we hang on the walls. But if scripture is the word of God, should it not do more? Should it not be the foundation on which the house itself is constructed, the concrete pillars on which it stands firm?

So if we select Psalm 24:7-10 to give us guidance on this occasion, we should read the passage carefully and allow its message to sink in. We should listen to the words, search their deepest meaning, pray over them. We should try to feel what the original author felt so that we imbue the emotional value no less than the intellectual contents. To understand the passage more fully, we turn to other texts which throw light on the same theme. In other words: Before determining the end result of our meditation, we allow the scriptural text—or more accurately, God through the text—to have his full say. Normally this requires time. If we have to preach, we do well to leave some space between the initial study of the text and the finalization of the homily. This time span is for mulling things over, for allowing vague impressions and deep stirrings to gell into a concrete message.

Of course, we do not forget, even at the beginning stage, to consider the other end of the spectrum: the pastoral needs of the audience. God's word will be addressed to a particular group of people. It will have to be relevant to this new context. We will, therefore, also reflect on the role a church building can play in a Christian community. We remember the special needs of the particular group for whom the church will serve as place of worship and apostolate. We will ask ourselves which aspects of the consecration event will be most important to them.

The two sources of reflection, the scriptural input and the pastoral concern, will influence each other. As the matter matures, points of contact will become clear. The outline of the message will suddenly emerge. It will then be a question of some further deepening and working out. The time has now come for putting the ideas into words. The homily can take its final shape.

Creative Musings

As I said before, the precise outcome of this process of guided rumination is unpredictable. If we give it free rein, we will feel the thrill of new discovery and genuine creative work. We will also find out that the word of God is truly alive and has a lasting message of vital interest.

Let us, for the sake of getting the feel of what I mean and for the sheer fun of it, imagine we are back in your liturgical committee. You have had another talk with your parish priest and he agrees now that he initially overreacted. Psalm 24 can be used after all. The committee has assembled and all of you share your feelings and thoughts. We witness a sermon being shaped in the womb!

"Taking Psalm 24:7-10 as our point of departure, let us try to fathom what the passage is really saying.... 'That the king of glory may come in....the mighty, the strong....' Why would God, present on the ark, be called the king of glory? Glory refers to majesty. Could God's majesty be seen as he entered the Temple, as it were, sitting on the ark?"

"Yes, the ark did inspire terror. It caused havoc among the Philistines. Uzzah was struck down on the spot when he reached out and touched the ark with his bare hand. Even the Levites serving in the Temple were forbidden to look into the ark, on pain of death. People in the Old Testament were afraid of the ark, of God's majesty....They always thought they would die in God's presence. Isaiah was totally overwhelmed when he saw God's glory....Does this still have validity for Christians?"

"In one way it doesn't. God is a God of love. Perfect love drives out all fear. But in another way, we still need to be reminded of God's majesty, of his greatness....Isn't that also the purpose of the church building: to underline the need of making space for God in one's life?...Are people really sufficiently aware of God's majesty? Would their prayers in church and their participation in the liturgy not be far deeper if they were overwhelmed by a sense of God's greatness? Has God become too familiar, so familiar in fact that he no longer fills us with awe and respect? What did Chesterton say: 'Take not thy thunder from us, but take away our pride.'...Yes, we should somehow discover again that God is a tremendous reality and that our church is a symbol of that reality...."

"At the same time, we should not forget the other side of God. What people need most is to be inspired by God's love. The church should be a home. So many people are lonely, have no home where they feel secure and cared for. That's why they come to church. To be consoled by God....I wonder what scripture has to say about that? Oh yes, there are those beautiful passages expressing the same sentiment:

"How I love your Temple, LORD Almighty!
How I want to be there....
Even the sparrows have built a nest,
    and the swallows have their own home;
they keep their young near your altars,
    LORD Almighty, my king and my God" (Ps 84:1-3).

"The Temple is the mother of all nations. Psalm 23 says: 'I know that your goodness and love will be with me all my life; and your house will be my home as long as I live' " (v. 6).

"Yes, this also fits well with the New Testament idea that Jesus' Body is our real Temple. A church is one expression of Jesus being with us. The whole community is part of that Body of Christ which is the new Temple. And in this new Temple there is place for everyone: there are no strangers."

"Good gracious, we have a lot of material here. We will need to sift it, select what is most telling for this parish....Throughout we must hold on to the key idea that now, after the consecration of the church, the king of glory takes up his residence in our community...."

It will be noted that the mental ruminations that gestate and give birth to a homily have much in common with the imaginative elaborations that feature in scriptural reflection (see Chapter 9). Meditation and preaching are closely related. The fathers of the Church used to say to priests: "Whenever you preach, pass on to your people what you have seen in contemplation." The best homilies are those that explicate what lives in the deep, spiritual experience of believers.

12

Light for
Distant Nations

The Salarjung Museum in Hyderabad holds surprises for visitors in practically every display room. But nothing can equal the 17th century French chandelier in a hall full of hourglasses and clocks. Suspended from the ceiling by one gracious arm, the lamp cascades down in a waterfall of glittering pieces of crystal. I remember on one occasion looking at it and admiring its beauty. Suddenly there was an electrical power failure. The light died in all the crystal mirror images. Yet, the chandelier did not look drab and dull. For though the light from inside had gone, some light from the window reflected in the crystal pieces in a startlingly new way. It struck me then how beautiful things depend on light for their beauty, and that light can come from different sources. Without such light striking them from outside, beauty and color simply don't exist.

The same is true of human words. We may think that words carry meaning in themselves. But this is not so. The words we speak have meaning only because of the light of external circumstances that shine on them. Words are signs that obtain their specific meaning from the situation in which they are spoken, from their context. I would like to discuss the importance of this for our understanding of the Old Testament in this chapter. When we consider the context of a particular passage, we have to think not only of the original context but also of subsequent contexts in which the passage was read and understood. I will try to make this clear. Even though the topic may seem somewhat academic, it is, I assure you, of importance to our understanding of God's inspired words.

Context has sometimes been defined as the "comparison-field" in which we speak. Usually there are many comparison-fields that we have to take note of. Let us take an everyday example. The simple phrase "your time has come" can mean different things to different people. From the dictionary we know what it signifies in a general sort of way, but to really understand its meaning we need to know the context. A man condemned to death will be afraid to hear those words. A woman who is going to give birth will be extremely happy. A prisoner who has completed his sentence will dance with joy when hearing it. In Ezekiel, it indicates the end of God's patience:

> "An end is coming, the end is coming upon you! See it coming! The climax has come for you who dwell in the land! *The time has come*, near is the day: a time of consternation, not of rejoicing" (Ez 7:6-7).

For Jesus, "the hour has come" meant suffering, glorification and return to his Father. In all these cases the phrase receives a different meaning from the comparison-fields within which it is spoken.

Or consider the following sentence from Isaiah: "You will be like a garden that has plenty of water" (Is 58:11). What does it mean to be like a garden that has plenty of water? If we lift this sentence out of its context, it could have unexpected connotations. For instance, in Holland much of the land lies low and is soggy and water-logged. A garden that has plenty of water poses a problem to the gardener: It requires extra expense to pump the water out. In that context, to be a garden with plenty of water is certainly not a compliment!

In China, on the other hand, people would smile at the expression. The phrase "plenty of water" would remind them of the burglar's proverb: Where there is plenty of water, there must be fish. This means that in a fine large mansion there are things worth stealing. To be a garden that has plenty of water means, therefore, to be rich, loaded with expensive articles that attract robbers and thieves!

In Andhra Pradesh this sentence might have yet another meaning. People familiar with Telugu literature will remember a warning from the Sumathi Shatakam poetry:

> Where property is assembed
> relatives will flock in.

> A pond with plenty of water
> will abound with frogs, will it not?

Again, a pointer to wealth, but now with reference to its social implications.

In the context of Isaiah, however, the connotations are different. Abundance of water is an advantage in a country that is dry and warm — the geographical comparison-field. Plenty of water remains one of the covenantal blessings — the religious comparison-field. The literary theme of closeness to water implies closeness to God (Ps 1:3; Jer 17:8) — the literary comparison-field. From such a study of the context of the original passage, we can understand that to become "a garden that has plenty of water" promises blessing and spiritual communion with God.

From all this we may draw a simple but important conclusion. Individual sentences should not be interpreted on their own. They have to be read in larger units: in paragraphs and chapters. For Isaiah 58, this means reading the whole unit consisting of verses 1-12. Moreover, we have to understand them within the larger context within which they were written. When we approach the Old Testament we should always study paragraphs or sections together. Only after having observed the meaning of the larger unit, and after having reflected on the comparison-fields implied, may we focus on individual phrases or statements. I already mentioned this in passing when discussing reflective reading. Now we know the reason for that recommendation. But there is more to come!

One Context After Another

In ordinary circumstances words have a limited life. They are spoken only once. They take their meaning from a particular context and that is it. They fade and are forgotten. But other statements we make take on new functions. When Napoleon was defeated in his Russian Campaign of 1812, he retreated to Warsaw where he met the French Ambassador, the Abbe' de Pradt. In a characteristic comment on his failure Napoleon said: "It is but one step from the sublime to the ridiculous." He meant that the sublime, a triumphant conquest of Russia, had been within his grasp and that his ignominious retreat was but one step removed from it. The phrase "from the sublime to the ridiculous" survived and is now widely used without people even knowing the original context. The phrase has acquired a life of its own. Many sayings entered the language in this way: "Can a leopard change its spots?" (Jer 13:23); "That is but cold comfort" (William Bradford, 1856); "All hope abandon, who enter here" (Dante Alighieri, 1314, about hell).

Larger chunks of literature can also acquire such a longer life. Many present-day English nursery rhymes began as political jingles. Here is one of them:

> Oh, the grand old Duke of York,
> He had ten thousand men.
> He marched them up to the top of the hill
> And marched them down again!
> And when they were up, they were up.
> And when they were down, they were down.
> And when they were only half-way up,
> They were neither up nor down.

The duke referred to in these verses was a historical person, a certain Frederick who fought in Belgium. But we don't know the exact battle the jingle refers to. One thing is certain: His contemporaries did not look upon him as a glorious general. Later, however, the verses were memorized and used to entertain children, one generation after the other. That is how they became a nursery rhyme. In our own days, fans of a football team, let us say in Yorkshire, could adopt it as their club song. In this way the old rhyme could take on the novel function of expressing the identity of this particular group. The rhyme thus has a number of meanings because of the different contexts in which it has been employed.

I am giving this kind of example because the same thing happened in the Old Testament. Certain passages that had been written down for a particular audience and that therefore had a well-defined meaning from that context, were later given a new meaning through a process of re-interpretation in a new context. The original author had a particular meaning in mind, but what God wanted to say may have exceeded that original intention. We need not be surprised about this. After all, God made use of these time-bound authors as his instruments, but he was speaking not only to their contemporaries, but also to later generations. Since relationship to the audience is part of the context and is an important comparison-field, God's message had, of necessity, to transcend the limitations of the situation of origin. This means that true scriptural meanings can be found in extensions of the original literal sense.

Let us look at a scriptural example:

> A voice cries out,
> "Prepare in the wilderness a road for the LORD!
> Clear the way in the desert for our God!"
> "Then the glory of the LORD will be revealed,
> and all mankind will see it" (Is 40:3,5).

The text is part of the vision of the new Exodus. The prophecies of Deutero-Isaiah (Is 40-55) were intended to comfort the people in exile with the promise of a new return to the Promised Land. The promise was fulfilled, in a way, when Jewish exiles returned from the countries where they had been in captivity and were actually allowed to go back to Palestine. But reflecting on the full meaning of the promises, the Isaian School of disciples realized that in the future God would fulfill his promises in an even more magnificent way. Thus the texts acquired their wider messianic meaning. It is on account of this wider messianic meaning that the early Christians could see how the vision had been realized abundantly, had been "fulfilled," in Jesus. In the words quoted about (Is 40:3,5) they could see it fulfilled even in such detail as the "voice in the desert," John the Baptist. And in a manner not imagined in the old prophecy it had come about in Jesus that "all mankind will see God's salvation" (Lk 3:6). This unexpected wider meaning of the prophecies is known as the fuller sense — fuller than understood in its earlier context, but not in contradiction to it. The fuller sense is homogeneous with, and an extension of, the literal sense.

Meanings That Go Beyond

The fuller sense is a deeper meaning intended by God even though the human authors did not clearly see it. The original seer who wrote about the "voice in the desert" could not possibly have foreseen that this would be fulfilled in John the Baptist's announcing the coming of Jesus. What we have to remember, though, is that this original seer was not the only seer of the passage. On account of the later re-reading and interpretation given by the disciples who followed, other persons became seers in the sense that they too gave the words new meaning. The same can be said, to some extent, of the Christians who started using the text in a christological way. In fact, as the text moved along, different people (new authors) used it in a different situation (a new context) with a different meaning (fuller sense).

A true fuller sense as I have described in this example is a limited phenomenon in the Old Testament. We can only speak with absolute certainty of such a fuller sense if we find that the interpretation is made explicit in later writings, especially in the New Testament. The texts involved usually carry messianic meanings and can be easily recognized by the way they are quoted in the New Testament. But there is another way in which the original literal meaning is extended: namely, through the way in which it can have a special meaning in our lives. This meaning, too, is intended by God, even though there is a subjective element in it. For when God inspired the scriptures, he also had us in mind. He wanted to address each one of us through these sacred words, and so he wanted them to have a special meaning within the context of our lives. This meaning we might call the *applied literal sense*. It is this specific meaning a text has for a particular person, the message from God for him or her. Obviously, this meaning must be based on the literal sense, but it goes beyond the literal sense because the message is now addressed to this particular person.

For instance, the words of Isaiah quoted earlier could have special meaning for someone who is reflecting on his life. "A voice cries out, 'Prepare in the wilderness a road for the Lord!' " Imagine that the person in question has grown careless in religion and now feels a new desire to experience God. Reading scripture he comes upon this passage. It suddenly may dawn on him that the text applies to him in a special way. The prophecy promises that God will come, but demands preparation. "Prepare a road for the Lord!" Translated to the person's situation this indicates God's reassurance that he will reveal himself, but also that the person may go through a desert of penance and silence. The person concerned realizes he will need to sort things out. He will have to fill the valleys and level the hills. This kind of interpretation is not fanciful speculation; it is exactly what the prophecy wants to say. But the original meaning is now actualized in the context of this person's life. This applied literal sense is genuinely scriptural; it is God's word speaking here and now.

Biography of a Chant

Now let us turn to a more complicated example. Psalm 45 was composed as a royal wedding song. It describes how the bride is led to the king:

> The princess is in the palace—how beautiful she is!
> Her gown is made of gold thread.
> In her colorful gown she is led to the king,
> followed by her bridesmaids (Ps 45:13).

The psalm seems to point to a historical wedding. The bride is from another nation (v.10), perhaps from Tyre or Sidon (v.12). The description of the king's palace (v.8) and the bride's wedding gown (v.13) are too detailed to be poetic fancy. Many authors believe the occasion was the wedding between King Ahab of Israel and Jezebel, the daughter of the king of Sidon (1 Kgs 16:31). This was the original context.

The wedding was also a religious event. The song was probably composed by a Levite, a singer attached to a sanctuary. After the wedding, the song may have been preserved within a body of sacred chants. Later it was used as a religious song itself. When it began to be sung in Temple, it acquired a new religious meaning. The king whose praises are sung— "You are the most handsome of men" (v.2)—was gradually understood to be the future Messiah. "The kingdom that God has given you," addressed to the king (v.6), was now read as "Your kingdom, O God." The bride may have been looked upon as a personification of God's wisdom as in Proverbs 8:1-31. The song was spiritualized in this sanctuary context.

After the coming of Christ, many Old Testament passages were seen in a new light. The early Christians knew that the Old Testament had served to prepare for Christ's coming. In this context of Christian reinterpretation the whole psalm was applied to Christ himself. The letter to the Hebrews quotes Psalm 45:6-7 as speaking of Christ:

> About the Son, however, God said:
> "Your kingdom, O God, will last forever and ever!
> You rule over your people with justice" (Heb 1:8).

In later centuries Christian devotion took a special fancy to the bride introduced in the second half of the psalm. The psalm was selected for liturgies in honor of Mary, St. Agnes, St. Anne, St.

Cecilia and of holy virgins in general. The words about the bride
were quoted and amplified in antiphons. Again it required a new
meaning, this time in a Christian liturgical context.

It is not the end of the story. The psalm can be recited with
relevance by people in our own times. A sister who is taking her
religious vows may well feel that God is speaking to her in words
such as:

> Bride of the king, listen to what I say—
> Forget your people and your relatives.
> Your beauty will make the king desire you;
> he is your master, so you must obey him (Ps 45:10-11).

Someone else may feel inspired by the opening words of the psalm:

> Beautiful words fill my mind
> as I compose this song for the king (Ps 45:1).

It could be the beginning of a personal prayer of praise and
thanksgiving. Such meanings are acquired by the text in our contemporary context.

To recapitulate what we have seen regarding Psalm 45, the
following table may be useful:

Time	Context	Who Is the King?	Who Is His Bride?
700 B.C.(?)	original, secular	A king of Israel (Ahab?)	A foreign queen (Jezebel?)
400-100 B.C.	sanctuary	the Messiah	personified Wisdom of God
A.D. 30-100	Christian reinterpretation	Jesus Christ	not specified
A.D. 500-1500	liturgical	Jesus Christ	Our Lady or a holy virgin
1980s	contemporary	Jesus Christ	religious sister

This analysis, obviously, is rather incomplete and crude, but it serves the purpose of showing that different contexts do produce new meanings. The question is: Are all these meanings inspired? It is clear that we have to make some distinctions here. The messianic interpretation that arose in the Israelite sanctuary and among the early Christians belongs to the fuller sense. It is truly scriptural, as is confirmed by its quotation in Hebrews 1:8-9. The association of the bride with Mary or with another saint, however, is an accommodated sense. It is not scriptural in the true sense of the word. The contemporary application to an individual's vocation is an applied literal sense. This too is meant by God. All this seems rather complicated. In practice, however, we will not find it so difficult to distinguish these various meanings.

Among the various contexts that matter for Old Testament texts, three stand out. The original context gives rise to the literal meaning. The context of Christian interpretation frequently brings out the fuller sense. Our own contemporary context determines how the literal sense is applied to our own life. As a rule of thumb, it is often useful to examine a text from the point of view of these three contexts.

Deutero-Isaiah was aware he had received a wide commission:

> Listen to me, distant nations,
>   you people who live far away!
> Before I was born, the LORD chose me
>   and appointed me to be his servant.
> The LORD said to me,
> "...I will also make you a light to the nations—
>   so that all the world may be saved" (Is 49:1,6).

Looking at the long history of his prophecies and how they inspired people through the centuries, from post-exilic Jews to Jesus himself and countless generations of Christians, we may confirm that the author did not fully realize how far his light would shine!

13

Flowers, Cedars and Mustard Trees

I read some time ago—I forget where—that a vehement discussion raged in Oxford University on the proposition, "It is useless to grow flowers." Growing flowers was an utter waste, some scholars maintained, because flowers do not produce anything substantial; for instance, they cannot be eaten. On reflection I am grateful that the Creator of the universe thought otherwise. How much poorer our world would be if all our plants were lettuces, beans and cabbages. There is something indescribably beautiful in the fragrance and freshness of daisies and daffodils, something which we do not find anywhere else. And what we express by flowers is also special. They bring a rainbow of colors to our house. They give a spark to a woman's hair. They add love to a gift of honor.

When we try to capture the meaning of realities such as flowers, we are in the realm of what was called *rasa-dhvani* in Indian literature. Understanding it may help us savor scripture, also the Old Testament. *Rasa-dhvani* was first recognized and explained by Anandavardhana of Kashmir in the 9th century.[1] I will try to outline the main characteristics of *rasa-dhvani* and show how it can help us appreciate Old Testament texts.

But we will start with the New Testament. Recall Jesus' well-known words on the lilies of the field:

> "Look how the wild flowers grow: they do not work or make clothes for themselves. But I tell you that not even King Solomon with all his wealth had clothes as beautiful as one

---

1. The full details of his theory are intricate and beyond the scope of this book. They can be studied in the excellent exposition of *Biblebhashyam*, Vol. 5, No. 4 (December, 1979).

of these flowers. It is God who clothes the wild grass — grass
that is here today and gone tomorrow, burned up in the
oven. Won't he be all the more sure to clothe you?" (Mt
6:28-30).

The literal meaning of Jesus' words concerns trust in God. He
teaches that we can expect God to look after us. But much more
is contained in the text if we allow its inner feelings, its heart,
to speak to us. This meaning (*rasa-dhvani*) is hinted at, is implied
in what Jesus says. It is difficult to express it in words, even
though it can be clearly perceived. Let me try to verbalize it this
way: As Jesus speaks we feel his great admiration for his Father.
God, in Jesus' view, looks at the whole of nature with infinite
tenderness and concern. To show his love he dresses the various
plants, even the wild grass, with exquisite and delicate flowers.
This inner feeling about the Father is the *dhvani*, the "sound,"
which reverberates through Jesus' words. When we listen to his
message we should not only take note of its explicit teaching (the
literal meaning) but should also savor the inner vibrations (the
suggested meaning, the *rasa-dhvani*) it contains.

Anguish of Love

To test this approach on the Old Testament, we might study
the following complaint:

> The LORD said, "Earth and sky, listen to what I am saying!
> The children I brought up have rebelled against me. Cat-
> tle know who owns them, and donkeys know where their
> master feeds them. But that is more than my people Israel
> know. They don't understand at all."
>
> "Why do you keep on rebelling? Do you want to be pun-
> ished even more? Israel, your head is already covered with
> wounds, and your heart and mind are sick. From head to
> foot there is not a healthy spot on your body. You are
> covered with bruises and sores and open wounds. Your
> wounds have not been cleaned or bandaged. No medicine
> has been put on them" (Is 1:2-3,5-6).

The whole oracle (Is 1:2-9) condemns Israel as a "corrupt and
evil people" (v.4). Yet God's tender love shines through his exasperation. Only a loving father could describe Israel's wounds
in such sorrowful and compassionate words. Noticing this *rasa-
dhvani* is more important than just paying attention to the ex-

ternal message. Without it we would miss what God is really trying to say. Having become aware of the *rasa-dhvani* we will now ask: Is God, perhaps, expressing his love for Israel in this way? Reflecting on the text again, we see it confirmed in God's punishment itself. God seems a hard master when he punishes his people. But in reality it is a sign of love. Israelite law allowed parents to hand over a rebellious son to the leaders of the town. These would then stone him to death. God does not want this to happen to his child, so he takes upon himself the slow and ungrateful task of personal correction. He is a loving father precisely because he is prepared to punish, and punish again.

A Father's Exasperation

At times the suggested meaning, the *rasa-dhvani*, is just the opposite of the explicit meaning. In the following discussion with Isaiah, God seems to be determined to destroy Israel:

> So he [God] told me to go and give the people this message: "No matter how much you listen, you will not understand. No matter how much you look, you will not know what is happening." Then he said to me: "Make the minds of these people dull, their ears deaf, and their eyes blind, so that they cannot see or hear or understand. If they did, they might turn to me and be healed."
>
> I asked. "How long will it be like this, Lord?"
>
> He answered, "Until the cities are ruined and empty — until the houses are uninhabited — until the land itself is a desolate waste" (Is 6:9-11).

The literal meaning of the prophecy answers the question: How can people be so deaf, so dull and so blind that they don't heed the prophet's warnings? Because God has made up his mind that they should be punished! But underlying this discussion we find another level of meaning, hinted at by the phrase, "they might turn to me and be healed." If Israel were to turn back with sorrow and contrition, God in his goodness would not be able to refuse forgiveness! Through this suggested meaning, the *rasa-dhvani*, we discover God's real intention, which is that Israel be converted and forgiven. The whole passage, therefore, expresses both God's willingness to forgive and the mystery of people's blindness.

Jesus himself had meditated on these verses and had drawn the conclusion that people's blindness had to be accepted as a fact.

When the disciples ask him why he teaches through parables, he replies:

"You have been given the secret of the Kingdom of God. But the others, who are on the outside, hear all things by means of parables, so that,
    'They may look and look,
      yet not see;
    they may listen and listen,
      yet not understand.
For if they did, they would turn to God
and he would forgive them!' " (Mk 4:11-12).

A superficial reading of these verses (see also Mt 13:14-15 and Lk 8:10) might give the impression that Jesus taught in parables to *hide* the meaning from the ordinary people. But that would be far from Jesus' intention and from that of the prophecy he quotes. No, Jesus has understood the *rasa-dhvani* of the oracle and knows God is anxious to show mercy. But the people are blind and deaf and dull. So unfortunately he cannot speak directly to them, as he could to his disciples. He has to speak in parables, hoping that their eyes and ears will gradually be opened.

The unbelief of the Jews was interpreted by the early Christians in the light of Jesus' understanding of Isaiah 6:9-11. John quotes the prophecy to reflect on the extraordinary blindness of the scribes and Pharisees: "Even though he had performed all these miracles in their presence, they did not believe in him" (Jn 12:37, cf.vv. 36-41). Paul refers to the same Isaian oracle when addressing the unbelieving Jews in Rome (Acts 28:24-28). There is no question in any of these texts of God being at fault, as if he did not want Israel to believe. No, what they mean to say is this: Don't be surprised to find unbelief. God himself is anxious that Israel be converted, yet he told Isaiah to be prepared for people's blindness. And what God told Isaiah applies to Jesus too. "Isaiah said this because he saw Jesus' glory and spoke about him" (Jn 12:41).

Finely Tuned Perception

To fully appreciate Jesus' sayings we often need to go back to the Old Testament texts that inspired him and to their heart, their *rasa-dhvani*. When the townspeople accuse Jesus of doing fewer miracles in Nazareth than in Capernaum, he replies:

Listen to me: "it is true that there were many widows in
Israel during the time of Elijah, when there was no rain
for three and a half years and a severe famine spread
throughout the whole land. Yet Elijah was not sent to
anyone in Israel, but only to a widow living in Zarephath
in the territory of Sidon" (Lk 4:25-26).

When we turn to the Old Testament story, we actually find a different stress in the text. God tells Elijah: "Go to Zarephath....I
have commanded a widow who lives there to feed you" (1 Kgs
17:9). In the book of Kings, God is concerned about Elijah; he
wants his prophet to survive. But Elijah's coming to Zarephath
saves the widow and her son from starvation and leads to the
miraculous raising of the son from death. Though the literal
meaning speaks of feeding the prophet, the *rasa-dhvani* points
to the special mercy shown to the widow.

Jesus had meditated on this inner meaning. Why had God
reserved this favor to a stranger, to someone outside God's people? Because God found more faith in her than with anyone
among his own people. Similarly, the Syrian Naaman had more
faith than the lepers of Israel. That is why he, not they, was
cured. The inner meaning led Jesus to recognize that "a prophet
is never welcomed in his home town" (Lk 4:24). It helped him
cope with the lack of faith among his relatives and family. He
was sad about it, but through *rasa-dhvani* he knew that Elijah
and Elisha had felt the same sadness.

Again, we need to be aware of the *rasa-dhvani* in one of Ezekiel's
loveliest poems, a poem singing the greatness of Egypt:

"You are like a cedar in Lebanon,
With beautiful, shady branches,
A tree so tall it reaches the clouds....
Every kind of bird built nests in its branches;
The wild animals bore their young in its shelter;
The nations of the world rested in its shade.
How beautiful the tree was—
So tall, with such long branches.
Its roots reached down to the deep-flowing streams.
No cedar in God's garden could compare with it.
No fir tree ever had such branches,
And no plane tree had ever such limbs" (Ez 31:3, 6-8).

The second half of the oracle announces God's intention, regret-
fully, to cut down the tree because of its wickedness. But the

description of the tree has its own *rasa-dhvani*. We feel the prophet's awe and admiration when faced with such a marvelous creation as a cedar of Lebanon. He finds it majestic, splendid, beautiful. It is overwhelming, like ancient Egypt with its palaces, temples and pyramids. His wonder and pleasure in seeing such splendor is clear. The kingdom of Egypt was as overpowering a creation of God as a mighty cedar of Lebanon!

It is only when we have internalized this *rasa-dhvani* that we get the right feel of Jesus' parable:

> "What shall we say the Kingdom of God is like? What parable shall we use to explain it? It is like this. A man takes a mustard seed, the smallest seed in the world, and plants it in the ground. After a while it grows up and becomes the biggest of all plants. It puts out such large branches that the birds come and make their nests in its shade" (Mk 4:30-32).

A mustard tree is not a cedar of Lebanon. Jesus undoubtedly chose the former for the parable, because its seed was proverbially small and because it was an ordinary plant in Palestine. But in Jesus' eyes, the plant truly becomes a tree and, with some poetic exaggeration, assumes the properties of a cedar. The kingdom of God, too, though small in the beginning will become so big as to inspire awe and admiration.

Our human mind has the power to transcend material reality and grasp lasting values underlying it. We can perceive beauty, greatness, harmony, dignity, tenderness, and similar values. It is this same ability which enables authors to incorporate *rasa-dhvani* in their writings, and which allows us to discover and savor it. It opens a level of communication all its own and all the more exciting when we are dealing with a text God is using to communicate with us!

14

Adrift on the Deluge of Living

After reading the previous chapters you may have the impression that the Old Testament functions as a storeroom full of useful decorations. Dusted and polished these serve well to illustrate truths of faith, you may think. They add an interesting dimension. They even throw unexpected light on familiar topics. They do well for festive sermons and learned conferences. But could they change our whole attitude to life? Can they give us profound new insights? Can they change us into more committed believers?

Yes, they can. It is unfortunate that many people have lost the ability to read the Old Testament the way it was meant to be: a book affecting the very texture of our existence. This is what I want to talk about in this chapter. The Bible is a book which can help us discover some of the deepest mysteries of our human life.

From the earliest times men and women have been speculating about the questions of existence. What drives this world in which we live? How did we come to be? Who made us? What is the purpose of birth, growth and death? Who or what determines whether we will be happy or not? What is the meaning of sickness and suffering? These questions are as valid today as they were a million years ago. They are still at the heart of religion. They are the real questions which every person, implicitly or explicitly, is seeking to answer. In a way, every person's life can be seen as an attempt to make sense of these questions.

As Christians we believe that we have some specific answers. We derive them from revelation. But these answers have no life-giving power if those to whom they are offered have not become consciously aware of the existential questions. Only the true seeker can fully appreciate and embrace the light of the gospel. Moreover, the answers indicated in the good news message do not destroy the mysteriousness of the original questions. They do not clear away fogs and mists; they give a beacon guiding us through fogs and mists. Christians are still intrigued by the mystery of life's deepest questions, but we walk forward confidently because we have been shown the right direction. Revelation does not blunt our human sensitivity to mystery; it refines our sense of wonder.

Despotic Waters

I was in India in 1977 just when the infamous cyclone hit the coastal region of Krishna district. A succession of waves rolled in from the ocean, some of them 60 feet high and moving 30 miles inland. It was just as if the sea had lifted itself to blot out the coastal strip. Sugar cane plantations, rice fields and roads were swamped; clumps of palm trees, farm houses, even whole villages, were hurled down and swept away. Fourteen-thousand people were killed. Two days later most of the water had receded. I remember the images vividly: desolation and swamps of mud as far as the eye could see, corpses of animals and of human beings in the most unlikely places. It raised all the fundamental questions: Why here? Why were these people hit while others escaped? What is the reason for this destructive power that can crush human life so unexpectedly?

In an attempt to answer these questions, primitive societies formulate stories which we call myths. A myth usually narrates the deeds of gods and goddesses. Though speaking of past events, it expresses a view on the present condition of the world. A myth gives a commentary on the nature of the universe in the form of a story. Sacred Scripture too contains myths. Their purpose is undoubtedly to make us think about the why and the wherefore of our existence.

Mankind sinned, we are told, and God was sorry he had created humanity. To give people a new chance, God decided to blot out the whole human race through an enormous flood. Only Noah and his family were saved. God warned him to build an ark. God told him to take a pair of each species of animal. Then God locked the ark and opened the sluices of heaven. The flood came down and covered the whole earth. After five months the water receded slowly. A full year after the flood had begun, Noah and his family left the ark to start a new life. They offered sacrifice and God concluded a covenant with them. The story covers three chapters in the book of Genesis (Gn 6-9).

The story of the deluge was a well-known myth in the ancient Middle East. We find a perfect parallel in the much older Gilgamesh epic. It is basically the same story; only the names are different. Instead of Yahweh, it is the assembly of the gods which decides to destroy mankind by a deluge. The man to be saved is not called Noah, but Utnapishtim. The ark grounded on Mount Nisar rather than Mount Ararat. Utnapishtim sends out three birds, as Noah did. He offers sacrifice when he leaves the ark and obtains the promise that the deluge will never happen again. There are some small variations, but by and large it is the same narration.

The myth also existed among the Hurrians and the Hittites. A fragmentary version of it has been found in Sumerian literature as well. The hero saved from the deluge in this case carries the name of Ziusudra. Then there is a Greek version of the myth. Deucalion, king of Phthia, was warned by his father Prometheus that Zeus intended to destroy the human race through a flood. He built an ark which saved his life and that of his wife Pyrrha. After some time Deucalion was reassured by a dove that dry land had reappeared. His ark landed on Mount Parnassus.

These examples illustrate that we are dealing here with a real myth, a myth that was known to practically all nations of the ancient Near East. Sacred Scripture has integrated the same myth. How closely it followed the original account can be seen from a comparison of the following section from the Gilgamesh story with Genesis 8:6-12:

> Mount Nisir held the ship fast,
>   allowing no motion.
> When the seventh day arrived,
> I sent forth and set free a dove;
>   since no resting-place for it was visible,
>   she turned round.
> Then I sent forth and set free a swallow.
> The swallow went forth, but came back;
>   since no resting place for it was visible,
>   she turned round.

> Then I sent forth and set free a raven.
> The raven went forth
> and, seeing that the waters had diminished,
> he eats, circles, caws, and turns not round
> (*Gilgamesh*, XI, 145-154).

Noah, too, sends out three birds: a raven, a dove and again a dove. Obviously, the inspired authors of this passage in Genesis (both the Jahwist and Priestly Code made use of the story), did some editing to fit the myth into their own Israelite belief. This too can be seen from comparing the Genesis version with the non-Hebrew versions of the myth.

Then I let out to the four winds	So Noah went out of the boat with his wife, his sons and their wives.
and *offered a sacrifice*. I poured a libation on the top of the mountain. Seven and seven cult-vessels I set up; upon their potstands I heaped cane, cedarwood and myrtle.	Noah built an altar to the LORD; he took one of each kind of ritually clean animal and bird, and *burned them whole as a sacrifice* on the altar.
The gods smelled the savor. The gods *smelled the sweet savor*. The gods crowded like flies about the sacrificer...	The *odor of the sacrifice pleased* the LORD, and he said to himself: "Never again will I destroy all living beings ...."
—*Gilgamesh*, XL, 155-161	—*Genesis* 8:18, 20-21

The biblical storytellers have used their own words. They describe the sacrifice in Jewish terms. It is Yahweh who smells the sweet odor, and so on, but essentially it is the same myth they retell.

Plumbing the Depths

It is important to notice all this because it gives us a clue as to how the narration should be understood. It is so easy to get stuck on the level of detail. The biblical authors do make small theological points here and there. The priestly author, for example, cannot resist the temptation to give a preferential treatment to "clean" animals: seven pairs of each kind are saved, he says, while the unclean animals escape with just one pair each (Gn 7:2). The Jahwist sticks to one pair of each kind, whether clean or unclean (Gn 6:20; 7:8-9). We are not surprised about this idiosyn-

cracy of the priestly code version; it never loses an opportunity
to inculcate fidelity to the Law. It recommends, in passing,
adherence to the laws on clean and unclean animals. But this
digression on the privileged status of clean animals is only an
aside, an extra, which should not distract us from the main purpose of the myth.

We should also refuse to be sidetracked by questions of historicity. Some commentators maintain that the myth must have arisen
on account of a real event. The tradition of a huge flood is also
found among African tribes and in Asian folklore, they say.
Perhaps, there is a trace here of what happened at the close of
the last Ice Age approximately 10,000 years ago. An enormous
amount of ice and snow on all the continents melted and was
released into the seas and oceans. The water level around the
globe rose at least 450 feet, submerging many of the coastal areas.
That memories of such catastrophic floods were retained in
primitive traditions is, indeed, an exciting possibility. Still, this
line of study, however interesting from a palaeontological point
of view, does not help us to enter into the myth itself. It is like
asking whether the parable of the Good Samaritan was based on
a historical incident. Even if it were, the parable remains a
parable and should be read as such.

So, how should we read a myth? As stated above, a myth reflects
our human condition in the form of a narrative. A myth speaks
about life. It makes us look at the world in which we live and
says to us: "See, have you noticed this or that? How does it affect
you? Have you ever considered that such or such a circumstance
could explain your condition? What are you going to do about it?
Will you willingly align yourself to this state of affairs, or are
you going to resist? Do you believe you can alter the facts of your
existence?" To allow the myth to address us in this way, we have
to let it tell its story without interruption. We have to let it vent
its emotions on us, so to speak, get at us with the deep feelings
it evokes. We have to make ourselves vulnerable to the unset-
tling questions it raises, to the razor-sharp edge of its challenge.
In short, we have to let the myth take over for just a short while.

Many of us are so superficial and trite because we have lost this
capacity of immersion into the elemental forces of our existence.
Formerly, people followed the cycle of nature in reliving the basic
myths of death and life, of winter and a new spring, of failure

and fertility, of loneliness and of participation with all the powers of nature. Could it be that this is the reason why in Western countries esoteric groups and magic cults have begun to flourish again, simply because the need to experience the limits of existence is so strong? The pagan rites with their stark ritual and mysterious myths gave people a chance to meet the original life-forces face to face. They were then inebriated with them. They were numb with fear, or they danced the ecstatic dance of spring and joy. As the myths spoke to them on the revolving occasions of the year, people relived their terror, their exuberance and the hope they offered. The church, too, presents us with a cycle of expectation, birth, penance, death and resurrection in its liturgical year. The myths are all there, as dramatic as they have ever been, but our failure to enter wholeheartedly into them has reduced their powers of release and revival.

The way to approach a myth, such as the deluge story, is to sit back in silence and go through the successive scenes in our imagination. We do not only observe what happens — as if we are looking in from the outside—but we know ourselves to be in the midst of the events. We do not just digest each new situation with our minds, but we also feel the deep emotions it provokes in the marrow of our bones. In the myth of the flood we pass through these scenes:

> People all around us go on enjoying life, doing what they like, suppressing others for their own gain. But God has made up his mind to destroy them all. Noah begins to build the ark. With alarm we feel the presentiment of the disaster, the threat of punishment while people fritter away their lives, laughing and joking.
>
> We see the tornadoes and cyclones that begin the flood. Dykes burst, rivers overflow, the water rises everywhere forming violent torrents in some places, a relentlessly choking mass of water in others.
>
> There is no escape. People climb on top of their houses, try to reach highland and mountains; the water pursues and drowns them wherever they go. We are terrified of this all-consuming, faceless, irresistible monster engulfing us on all sides.
>
> With Noah in the ark we are seasick and fearful, yet strangely secure and resigned. The rolling and heaving of the ship, the battering of heavy rain on the top deck reminds us constantly of the

dangers without. So we endure the confinement which the vessel imposes upon us; we feel somehow attached to the ark even though it is a prison at the same time. Though narrow and constricting, it has become our secure home.

We leave the ark a new people. How glorious the whole world looks in spite of the recent disaster! We sing; we breathe in the fresh air; we promise to build a new earth; we embrace each other in unspeakable joy when God says he will never bring on a deluge again.

No thinking mind, no human heart can remain untouched as we move through these events. Our inner self reverberates, because it recognizes elements of its own existence, shreds of deep, personal experience. It is here that we must let our response take its own course. To be real it will have to link up with the associations that stir us most. The deluge myth has an overall scheme, of course, but its real power lies in being able to give depth to our self-concept, to our attempt to make sense of our own life experiences. So, naturally, one aspect will speak most to this person, while another feels overcome by a second. A certain feature of the myth may fascinate us early in life; another one may have a hold on us as we grow older. The myth achieves its meaning not by imposing a uniform lesson, but by making individual people respond to fundamental experiences of life.

Oceans Of Threat

Jesus had obviously been impressed by the scene of impending disaster. His preaching of the kingdom fell on deaf ears. People turned away from his message of repentance with unbelief and indifference. Jesus felt sad and frustrated as he saw how people frittered away their lives in frivolous monotony and how they would do so till the day of judgment. The parallelism with the deluge myth, the menace of inescapable disaster, gripped him.

"The coming of the Son of Man will be like what happened in the time of Noah. In the days before the flood people ate and drank, men and women married, up to the very day Noah went into the boat; yet they did not realize what was happening until the flood came and swept them all away. That is how it will be when the Son of Man comes" (Mt 24:37-39).

Jesus' words were spoken with sorrow, with regret that people could be so unconcerned about their own ultimate good. The deluge myth became the vehicle to perceive and express his own exasperation.

For Jews the sea was a very strong image of death and the powers of evil. The Jews were no seafaring nation; they feared the sea. In Semitic creation myths the sea was the original force of evil that needed to be defeated by the creator god in a bloody combat. Only God could keep the sea in check by laying down strict boundaries:

> Who closed the gates to hold back the sea
> when it burst from the womb of the earth?
> I marked a boundary for the sea
> and kept it behind bolted gates.
> I told it, "So far and no farther!
> Here your powerful waves must stop" (Jb 38:8,10-11).

Only God could provide security against the water's threat of evil and death:

> The ocean depths raise their voice, O LORD;
> they raise their voice and roar.
> The LORD rules supreme in heaven,
> greater than the roar of the ocean,
> more powerful than the waves of the sea (Ps 93:3-4).

The awareness of this conflict between the sea and God adds perspective to Jesus' walking on the water, to his stilling the storm. It makes us understand why the book of Revelation makes the Antichrist originate from the sea:

> Then I saw a beast coming up out of the sea (Rv 13:1).

It adds meaning to the beginning of chapter 21:

> Then I saw a new heaven and a new earth. The first heaven and the first earth disappeared, and the sea vanished (Rv 21:1).

With Peter we may dwell on the salvation of a few by the passage through water (baptism: 1 Pt 3:18), or with the Fathers we might compare the church to the ark that keeps us alive in a world full of death.

> Whoever leaves the Church, cannot benefit from Christ. He makes himself a stranger, a worldling, an enemy. Who does

not want the Church as mother, cannot have God as father. As little as anyone outside the ark of Noah could escape death, can anyone escape now who stays outside the Church?

—St. Cyprian, A.D. 251

I know the Church was built on that rock (on Peter)....If anyone will not have remained in Noah's ark, he will perish during the flood.

—St. Jerome, A.D. 379

It is the mystery of a fragile structure of planks lined with tar (Gn 6:14) turning out to be our only instrument of salvation! It is a thought fraught with theological and pastoral questions: How can a limited, human, fragile institution as the church serve such an important role in the storms of history?

These example from scripture and early Christian writers are not meant to restrict our own elaboration of the myth. They only give an idea of how the myth can take off in different directions. If we ponder the same myth, if we allow the cords of our heart to resonate in their own way, the myth will undoubtedly start its own train of thought and realize its own feelings. When we allow all this to crystallize itself out in meditation and prayer, the myth will have a lasting effect on our life. It will confirm us, or warn us, or fix our attention on something we might have overlooked.

There are quite a few myths in the Old Testament. Those concerning the origins of humankind and earliest history stand out. Others are found as traces in the psalms and in prophetic writings. Even the story of the Exodus from Egypt and the conquest of the Promised Land, though based on historical events, have acquired the quality of myth through their antiquity and primordial importance. It is not unlike the mythical power of Jesus' birth, death and his resurrection. Although these were historical events, the stories of these events have assumed the additional dimension of illustrating the fundamental values of our existence. They spell out the meaning of life.

Part Three

Roots of
Christian Discipleship

"Your ancient scriptures
lack the gospel values
which I love, Lord:
your beatitudes,
your kingdom parables,
your cross and resurrection,
the power of your Spirit!"

"Look again.
It's all there.
Like stem, branches,
leaves and flowers
folded in a seed!"

"Give me eyes that see
as you do.
Give me insight
and the perceptiveness
of your love."

15

Standing With Two Feet on God's Soil

For many people religion is an unreal world. When we say that Jesus is God, for example, it means little, for they have neither known Jesus as a human person nor ever seen God. Religious truths seem vague, mystic, abstract, far removed from the realities of life. Working to earn some money, keeping the house clean, preparing food, maintaining good relationships with the neighbors, these are true realities, tangible and immediate. The things we can see and the people we meet are the world we live in. The spiritual dimension of existence requires a special effort to believe — which is the reason why some give up, particularly when worries and challenges of concrete living demand their attention.

Once, during the Christmas season, I heard a sermon on the child Jesus which could be condensed in the following lines:

> The infant Jesus, even when only a small boy, radiated piety and virtue. He was always ready to help Mary and Joseph. He performed his duties happily. Though he was almighty God all the time, he did not mind being treated as a child. The power of the incarnation is seen clearly in the tiny limbs of this young child, yes, in the Babe of Bethlehem. Devotion to the child Jesus pleases God so much. The infant Jesus will not refuse us any favors we confidently ask when kneeling at his manger!

Talking like this, however well-intentioned, relegates faith to a world of fantasy. Who of us has actually seen the child Jesus at Nazareth? Can we really kneel before his manger in Bethlehem? For that matter, with what right can we speak of Jesus as a babe?

We may join preachers in condemning people for being short-sighted and lacking in faith. We may put the blame on secularism,

145

on the lure of material goods, on the godless society in which we
live. But is this a truthful response? Could it be that religion, or
at least our way of presenting it, *is* unreal? Do the spiritual and
the theological slogans we use carry a meaningful content – or are
they only part of some elaborate theoretical scheme? Could it be
that we are just mouthing words, repeating what others have
said before us, without saying anything definite that people can
put their finger on? What is the "cash value" of our message?

Religion in the Old Testament times was crude and primitive
in many respects. But at the same time there was a healthy
realism about it. Consider, for instance, the question of the covenant. The Jewish people knew that they lived in a special relationship with God.

> "You will be my chosen people, a people dedicated to me
> alone, and you will serve me as priests" (Ex 19:5-6).

> "You belong to the LORD your God. From all the peoples
> on earth he chose you to be his own special people"(Dt 7:6).

This special relationship, however, was not purely an imaginary
thing, something believed but not seen. They experienced its reality every day— because the spiritual awareness of being a chosen
people was linked to the tangible reality of living in the Promised
Land.

The land was the external sign of the covenant. When the
Israelite farmer walked through his vineyard or his field of barley,
he smelled and touched the presence of the covenant. His feet
stood firmly on its fertile soil. His hands felt its living pulse in
grapes and budding wheat. The blessings of the land were the
visible expression of God's covenantal love.

> "The land that you are about to occupy is not like the land
> of Egypt, where you lived before. There, when you planted
> grain, you had to work hard to irrigate the fields; but the
> land that you are about to enter is a land of mountains and
> valleys, a land watered by rain. The LORD your God takes
> care of this land and watches over it throughout the year.

> "So then, obey the commands that I have given you today;
> love the LORD your God and serve him with all your heart.
> If you do, he will send rain on your land when it is needed,
> in the autumn and in the spring, so that there will be
> grain, wine and olive oil for you, and grass for your live-
> stock. You will have all the food you want" (Dt 11:10-15).

When the covenant was broken, when God was angry because his people had been unfaithful to him, the effects could immediately be seen in the barrenness of the land. Without the covenant, the land refused to produce. Rainfall ceased and the ground became as hard as iron. Plentiful seed brought no more than a pitiful harvest. Locusts ate the corn and worms the vines. Diseases in the crops, dust storms, plagues of insects befell the land. Then the Israelites knew the covenant had been disturbed for God's "curse" was on the land (Dt 28:24,38-42). And if they failed to restore friendly relations with God, God would not stop at partial punishments. Infidelity to the covenant would eventually lead to God taking away the land altogether.

> "I call heaven and earth as witnesses against you today that, if you disobey me, you will soon disappear from the land."
>
> "The LORD will scatter you among other nations" (Dt 4:26,27).

Covenant and land were two sides of the same coin!

Visible Blessing

Linking sin to disaster and virtues to prosperity was bound to raise questions. Why do sinners prosper? Why do just people suffer? It was a problem for the Old Testament, but whatever answer was given, the principle of blessing and curse as tangible realities was not given up. Psalm 37 is highly instructive in this regard. Wicked people often prosper for some time, the psalmist concedes. Their evil plans succeed. They oppress the poor and needy. They borrow and do not pay back. But their triumph is short-lived. They cannot last because the land is hostile to them. The righteous man, on the other hand, who patiently endures injustices and sticks to his principles, will be rewarded because the land will be good to him. In the following quotations from Psalm 37, notice how possession of the land, living in the land, is the continual refrain of blessing.

> Trust in the LORD and do good;
> live in the land and be safe (v.3).
>
> Those who trust in the LORD will possess the land,
> but the wicked will be driven out (v.9).
>
> The humble will possess the land
> and enjoy prosperity and peace (v.11).

The LORD takes care of those who obey him,
and the land will be theirs forever (v.18).
Those who are blessed by the LORD will possess the land,
but those who are cursed by him will be driven out (v.22).
The righteous will possess the land
and live in it forever (v.29).
Put your hope in the LORD and obey his commands;
he will honor you by giving you the land (v.34).

The possession of the land in all these cases is not to be understood as a future gift. The humble possess it now. They survive trouble and persecution because the land is good to them.

They will not suffer when times are bad;
they will have enough in time of famine (v.19).
I am an old man now; I have lived a long time,
but I have never seen a good man abandoned by
the LORD or his children begging for food (v.25).

I interpret it in this way: At all times and in all circumstances the just experience that the land is good to them. And this goodness is the tangible proof of God's love and of his blessing. The just know God loves them because they feel the supportive protection of the land.

Like his contemporaries, Jesus was steeped in Old Testament thinking. He, too, must have felt the visible blessings of his Father when he walked on his native soil. That Jesus loved the land can be seen from the many parables he derived from it, parables about sowing and reaping and winnowing, about pruning vines and manuring olive trees. He admired the birds in the air and the wild flowers, a beautiful dress God gave to cover his land! But Jesus understood at the same time that the Father was offering a new land, a spiritual kingdom, instead of the initial Promised Land. This kingdom was the reality of messianic blessing, the kingdom which the humble were to possess. Jesus began to read Psalm 37 in a new light. It was from Psalm 37:11 that he derived the model for the first beatitude:

"Happy are those who know they are spiritually poor;
the Kingdom of heaven belongs to them!" (Mt 5:3).

Manifest Happiness

With our lack of Old Testament awareness, we have greatly undervalued, if not misunderstood, the meaning of Jesus' word.

The spiritually poor, we tend to think, are worthy of the kingdom. They will be rewarded with the kingdom—invisibly now (through God's grace working in them), visibly later in heaven. But then we forget the analogy with the land. The land was the visible and tangible sign of the covenant. So the kingdom of heaven, too, should be tangible and visible. What Jesus is promising to the "spiritually poor" is that they will know, see and touch the kingdom of God. They are happy, they are blessed, because they will actually experience that new land: the kingdom of his Father!

The kingdom was not an abstract notion for Jesus; it was something that could be seen. The Father's kingdom exists where there is true love between people; where people are ready to forgive each other; where people are merciful; where they live together in peace and friendship. The sign by which disciples of the kingdom are recognized is the love they have for one another. Other characteristics are the joy of generous giving, selfless service, being good to one's enemies, never taking revenge or reacting with violence. All this is not vague or abstract. It is something we can observe and recognize. It is the tangible presence of the new kingdom.

When we apply this to our own situation, the implications are startling. Suppose I meet a Christian community—a parish, inmates of an institution, members of a convent. How do I know that the kingdom of God is there? Not because it carries a Christian name. Nor because its leaders have a function in a Christian organization. Nor on account of the buildings or the customs Christians use. The reality of the kingdom lies not in such externals, but in the spirit pervading the community. Do I feel the love, mutual tolerance, open-mindedness, joyful service and fraternal peace required by Jesus? If so, I know the kingdom of God exists in this community. If not, for all its Christian pretense, the essence may be lacking.

The same holds true on a personal level. If I find religion an eerie and abstract dimension in my life, it may be that I have not discovered the reality of the kingdom. It is by the love I experience, the joy, the peace, the new relationships created by renouncing myself that I can know that God is truly present. I can feel his hand in the new world he has put me into. There is nothing abstract about this, nothing imaginary. It is only a matter of opening my eyes to its reality; of becoming sensitive to it; of noticing how much it can be part of my day-to-day existence and of all my relationships.

In the Old Testament the Israelites knew God's covenant was real because they felt the land under their feet. They tasted God's love and care when they ate their food. Christians, too, enjoy a similar directness in their religious experience. They see the kingdom of God in the quality of love that pervades the community to which they belong, the peace and joy that flow from the love they live.

16

Prophets and Witnesses
of Our Master

Some time ago when I was browsing through St. John's gospel, I came across these reassuring words of Jesus: "Whoever believes in me will do what I do — yes, he will do even greater things" (Jn 14:12). That is surely an exaggeration, I thought. It cannot be true. This has to be understood as hyperbolic language. Doing greater things than Jesus has done! But when I studied the context and began to think about it, the full impact of Jesus' statement dawned on me. Jesus meant what he said, and its message has weighty implications.

Jesus has just declared, "Whoever has seen me has seen the Father." He goes on to say that he is in the Father and the Father in him. Also his teaching is not his own teaching, but the Father's. Jesus' activity, in other words, what he does and says, reveals the Father. Then he continues:

> "The Father, who remains in me, does his own work. Believe me when I say that I am in the Father and the Father is in me. If not, believe because of the things I do. I am telling you the truth: whoever believes in me will do what I do—yes, he will do even greater things, because I am going to the Father. And I will do whatever you ask for in my name, so that the Father's glory will be shown through the Son" (Jn 14:10-13).

Whatever Jesus does—the preaching on the kingdom, the manifestation of his power, his service to the people—is all work done by the Father. In the same way the Father will work in Jesus' disciples. Jesus is going to heaven, but in the disciples the same work of the Father will go on. The disciples, therefore, will do what Jesus did—yes, even greater things than he did.

This Johannine definition of discipleship struck me so forceful-
ly because it shows that Christian discipleship is of a totally different nature than rabbinical discipleship. Jesus' disciples depend
on their master's words, as *talmidim* learn words from their *rab-
bi*. But there is a difference. The word becomes active in them.
They receive their own mission. They are Jesus' successors, rather
than only followers.

Not Less Than the Master

The true model for Christian discipleship can be found in prophetic succession. God tells Elijah, "Anoint Elisha son of Shaphat
from Abel Meholah to succeed you as prophet" (1 Kgs 19:16). The
account also tells us how Elisha was called.

> Elijah left and found Elisha plowing with a team of
> oxen; there were eleven teams ahead of him, and he was
> plowing with the last one. Elijah took off his cloak and put
> it on Elisha. Elisha then left his oxen, ran after Elijah, and
> said, "Let me kiss my father and mother good-bye, and then
> I will go with you."
>
> Elijah answered, "All right, go back. I'm not stopping you!"
>
> Then Elisha went to his team of oxen, killed them, and cook-
> ed the meat, using the yoke as fuel for the fire. He gave
> the meat to the people, and they ate it. Then he went and
> followed Elijah as his helper" (1 Kgs 19:19-21).

Commentators differ on this text. If I read the text correctly,
Elisha did not kiss his father and mother goodbye. He interpreted
Elijah's answer as a refusal. His new commission was far too important. So he made a meal with his oxen to indicate that his old
job was over.

The vocation stories in the gospel follow this pattern. This is
true of the way they are described, but also, I believe, of the way
Jesus himself approached the call. Like Elisha, the apostles are
called away from their jobs: Peter and Andrew from their fishing
boat, Matthew from the customs house. Jesus called them to a
prophetic task, not to classes about the Law. Great urgency speaks
from his stern demand of unconditional and immediate following — expressed in the three words of Luke 9:57-62, the last one
of which was obviously modelled on Elisha's vocation:

> Another man said, "I will follow you, sir; but first let me
> go and say good-bye to my family!"

> Jesus said to him, "Anyone who starts to plow and then keeps looking back is of no use for the Kingdom of God" (Lk 9:61-62).

If Jesus called successors as Elijah had done, it is worth studying the relationship between Elijah and Elisha. The actual handing over of power is described in an unusual narration. Elisha knows that Elijah will be taken up to heaven, so he stays close to his master. Eventually, when they have crossed the Jordan, Elijah asks what Elisha wants.

> "Let me receive the share of your power that will make me your successor," Elisha answered. "That is a difficult request to grant," Elijah replied. "But you will receive it if you see me as I am being taken away from you; if you don't see me, you won't receive it" (2 Kgs 2:9-10).

Elisha actually saw Elijah being taken away, and so he knew he had become the successor. He picked up the cloak which Elijah had dropped and performed the same miracle of dividing the water of the Jordan which Elijah had done previously. The subsequent deeds of Elisha demonstrate the same point. Elijah made a bowl of flour and a jar of oil last through a whole period of famine; Elisha miraculously multiplies a jar of olive oil; Elijah raised the dead son of a widow to life; Elisha does the same for the woman of Shunem. Elisha did the same marvelous things Elijah had done; yes, even greater things, because he cured Naaman the leper.

The gospels, of course, portray Jesus not only as the new Moses but also as the new Elijah. Jesus compares himself to Elijah and Elisha (Lk 4:25-27). Some of Jesus' miracles remind us of these prophets: his healing, the multiplication of the loaves, the raising of the widow's son. Most telling, perhaps, is the way Luke brings out that the disciples saw Jesus when he was taken away.

> As he was blessing them, he departed from them and was taken up into heaven (Lk 24:51).

> After saying this, he was taken up to heaven as they watched him, and a cloud hid him from their sight (Acts 1:9).

In the light of Elijah's words to Elisha, seeing Jesus being taken up to heaven confirmed the power of succession.

Elisha's request, translated as "the share of your power that will make me your successor," reads literally as, "Let me inherit the double share of your spirit." The double share was the right of the first son, the successor. Elisha, therefore, literally asked that he might inherit Elijah's spirit as his full successor. Again, we find the same theme repeatedly brought out in the gospel. Jesus passes on the Spirit to his disciples.

> "When, however, the Spirit comes, who reveals the truth about God, he will lead you into all the truth....He will take what I say and tell it to you" (Jn 16:13-14).

He breathed on his disciples and said, "Receive the Holy Spirit" (Jn 20:22). Because we have Jesus' Spirit, we have succeeded fully in his mission. "As the Father sent me, so I send you" (Jn 20:21). We have the double share of his Spirit!

How much Elijah's and Elisha's missions were intertwined may be seen from this observation. While Elijah was on the Sinai, God told him to anoint Hazael as king of Syria and Jehu as king of Israel. He received these orders before he called Elisha. He didn't execute either commission. It was Elisha who put them into operation. Elisha told Hazael he would be the future king of Syria. And Elisha sent one of the young prophets to anoint Jehu as the new king of Israel. Also in this way he proved that he was Elijah's true successor: He continued and completed the tasks that had been entrusted to his Master. In the same way we find that Jesus entrusted his own commission to the disciples. "Go, then, to all people everywhere and make them my disciples...teach them to obey everything I have commanded you" (Mt 28:19-20).

The Dignity of Sharing

What conclusions may we draw for these reflections? First of all, as Jesus' disciples we are not his servants, but his equals! This seems a daring assertion. Yet it is true. We can say, as Paul does, that we serve Jesus, that we are his servants. We say so because we help him, assist him, obey his instructions. But we may not say it with a feeling of inferiority, with a sense of misguided submissiveness. Just as Elisha, though a disciple, became Elijah's equal through succession, so we, too, have become real children of God and co-heirs with Christ. Christ is the first-born and "the only Son," yet all of us have become God's sons and daughters, Christ's brothers and sisters. That is why Christ does not consider us servants but friends, because "I have told you everything I heard from my Father" (Jn 15:15). We are Christ's equals.

It also follows that we are more than secretaries and copyists; we are prophets and witnesses. Not that we are called upon to invent a new message, a message that would deviate from Christ's. Rather we are called to continue his teaching, to enlarge it so that it becomes "the full truth," to make it develop so that it increases a hundredfold. We have to become teachers who can produce new and old things according to the requirement of our mission. We are exercising a prophetic teaching function and Christ will back us up: "Whoever welcomes you welcomes me" (Mt 10:40). Our prophetic message will so much be part of ourselves, that we can be called "witnesses" (Lk 24:48) and witnesses "filled with power" (Acts 1:8). Witnesses are not parrots who repeat someone else's thinking. Witnesses communicate what they themselves have seen and heard and are convinced about.

We are not just followers, but leaders. Followers play a secondary role. They put into practice what their master told them. They execute plans formulated by someone else. But Elisha was not Elijah's follower. He became a new leader in his own right. In the same way Christ makes us leaders in our own right. He has given us the initial capital: one, two or five talents. He expects us to enlarge that capital through our own creative skill and hard work. He wants his disciples to learn from the inventiveness and dedication of shrewd businessmen, even though they are "children of the darkness" (Lk 16:8). Whenever Jesus sends his disciples on a mission, he gives them a share in his power. Thus we become more than followers; we are enabled to carry out our tasks through a new source of power in us.

Equals to Christ; prophets and witnesses like him; leaders. This means that each disciple does to some extent become a new Christ. Discipleship implies full succession. It is here that the teaching in St. John's gospel becomes crystal clear: Jesus was filled with God; he was in his Father and his Father in him; no one has ever seen God, but Jesus made the Father known; Jesus' deeds revealed the Father; whoever saw Jesus, saw the Father. In the same way the Father will take full possession of the disciple. The Father loves such a person, comes to him and lives in him. The Father prunes such a person as the branch of a precious vine to make it bear fruit. The Father dedicates such a person to himself by means of the truth. The Father guides and strengthens such a person through the Holy Spirit. Just as Jesus was filled with the Father, so the disciple will be. That is why the disciple will do the great things Jesus did — yes, even greater things.

This also explains why Jesus can say that it is better for us that he goes.

> "If you loved me, you would be glad that I am going to the Father, for he is greater than I" (Jn 14:28).

> "I am telling you the truth: it is better for you that I go away, because if I do not go, the Helper will not come to you. But if I do go away, then I will send him to you" (Jn 16:7).

Though Elisha loved his master, it was better for him that Elijah was taken up to heaven. This was not only because it would give his master the reward he deserved, but also because only then could Elisha succeed to his master's task and receive "the double portion of his spirit." In the same way, it was better for Joshua that Moses was taken up to heaven.

Commissioned With a Conquest

Joshua, son of Nun, had been Moses' assistant since he was a young man. He stood by Moses in the rebellion of the ten spies. He led the people in the battle against the Amalekites. When Moses was going to be taken up to heaven, God told him to make Joshua his successor:

> "Take Joshua son of Nun, a capable man, and place your hands on his head. Have him stand in front of Eleazar the priest and the whole community, and there before all proclaim him as your successor. Give him some of your own authority, so that the whole community of Israel will obey him" (Nm 27:18-20).

Moses did as he was told. He encouraged Joshua with the words:

> "You are the one who will lead this people....The LORD himself will lead you and be with you. He will not fail you or abandon you, so do not lose courage or be afraid" (Dt 31:7-8).

Joshua was "filled with wisdom, because Moses had appointed him to be his successor" (Dt 34:9).

Joshua's greatest confirmation, however, came after Moses' death. For until that moment he had somehow derived all his authority from Moses. But now God himself spoke directly to Joshua and commissioned him to occupy the promised land, something Moses had not been able to do:

> "My servant Moses is dead. Get ready now, you and all the people of Israel....As I told Moses, I have given you and all my people the entire land that you will be marching over....Joshua, no one will be able to defeat you as long as you live. I will be with you as I was with Moses....Make sure that you obey the whole Law that my servant Moses gave you....Do not be afraid or discouraged, for I, the Lord your God, am with you wherever you go" (Jos 1:1,3,5,7,9).

If we turn to the end of St. Matthew's gospel, we will see that this was the scene Matthew had in mind. Moses saw the Promised Land from Mount Nebo, but he himself could not enter it. Jesus, too, saw all the nations of the earth but left their conquest to his successors. As Joshua was given power, so Jesus gave it to his disciples. As God would be with Joshua, so Jesus would be with his disciples "always, to the end of the age" (Mt 28:20). The disciples would be leaders in their own right as Joshua had been— in faithfulness to God's plan.

This commission, like other words through which Jesus conferred power, applies to his disciples in degrees. Through their specific ministry some partake more of one kind of authority, others of another kind. But the concept that discipleship implies succession, not merely dependence, applies equally to all Christians. The basic equality of all as Jesus' disciples, as second Christs in the world, is fundamental to Jesus' idea of the kingdom. All of us are called to be "the chosen race, the King's priests, the holy nation, God's own people, chosen to proclaim the wonderful acts of God" (1 Pt 2:9). Each one of us is to Christ what Elisha was to Elijah, what Joshua was to Moses.

17

Getting a Donkey
Back on Its Feet

Some time ago a young priest whom I had known as a seminarian, told me the following story:

When I left the seminary, I was full of ideals and good intentions. I was appointed to a village parish as assistant to an old parish priest. He is a good person, but one hundred per cent of the old school. He does not allow me to take any initiative. He does not want a parish council. He stopped me from starting a youth movement. When I visit people's homes, he is suspicious and asks questions.

At first I thought it was only the parish priest. Then I found the people did not want a change either. When I talked to the vicar general and some senior priests in the diocese, they advised me to keep quiet. "If you make too much noise," they said, "you will get the reputation of causing trouble. Just do your work as everybody else does." Thinking it over I found the whole system is against me. So I gave up trying, and now I am doing exactly what everyone else is doing.

A similar story could be told by many persons in different situations of life: by a teacher who would like to introduce changes into a school; by a religious sister who believes her congregation should adopt a different lifestyle; by a bishop who would like to have cordial relations with Protestant groups in his area. What they are up against is not just a lack of understanding in one or two persons, but a system. Each system is a network of beliefs, attitudes, traditions and established customs which it seems almost impossible to break down.

When we analyze such a system from a sociological point of view, we find that it rests on many explicit and implicit laws. The young priest mentioned earlier was actually facing dozens of rules of behavior, among them,

- We don't start new things in our parish.
- Young people should listen and conform.
- Priests should remain close to the church.
- The pastor is absolute lord and master.

Furthermore, the people imagine that the official laws of the church give support to these unwritten laws. They might say: "The bishop has appointed the pastor. Scripture teaches that young people should be humble and obey. The way our parish is run was laid down by the church." Thus the system is believed to be unshakable because it is based not only on customs and traditions, but ultimately on official laws and the will of God. How can one escape if God himself is part of the system?

Subversive Justice

When we study the law books of the Old Testament we make a remarkable discovery. Many of the laws seek to regulate social obligations, it is true; yet, in their essence, they aim at protecting and liberating people from the system. The laws do not support the system, but break through it.

Let us begin with an example from the economic order. In every human society there is a tendency for some families to become rich and others poor. The rich acquire power and do their utmost to strengthen their own position. A capitalistic system may emerge in which the rich hold most of the property and an absolute right to its use. The system, then, is a system of the rich.

Yet the economic laws of the Old Testament are laws for the poor. Consider the following:

> "If you lend money to any of my people who are poor, do not act like a moneylender and require him to pay interest" (Ex 22:25).

> "At the end of every seventh year you are to cancel debts of those who owe money. This is how it is to be done. Everyone who has lent money to a fellow Israelite is to cancel the debt. He must not try to collect the money; the LORD himself has declared the debt canceled" (Dt 15:1-2).

> "For six years plant your land and gather in what it produces. But in the seventh year let it rest, and do not harvest anything that grows on it. The poor may eat what grows there" (Ex 23:10-11).

> "Do not cheat a poor and needy hired servant....Each day
> before sunset pay him for that day's work; he needs the
> money and has counted on getting it. If you do not pay him,
> he will cry out against you to the LORD and you will be
> guilty of sin" (Dt 24:14-15).

> "When you walk along a path in someone else's vineyard,
> you may eat all the grapes you want, but you must not carry
> any away in a container" (Dt 23:24).

> "Do not show partiality to a poor man at his trial....Do not
> deny justice to a poor man when he appears in court" (Ex
> 23:3,6).

What is so interesting about these laws is that they upset the
absolute right over their property claimed by the rich. Lending
out money, for example, is not profitable if one cannot exact interest; it is especially risky if all debts are automatically can-
celed every seven years! This kind of lending contradicts the
natural instincts of every businessman. Yet the law states em-
phatically:

> "Be generous and lend him [the poor man] as much as he
> needs. Do not refuse to lend him something, just because
> the year when debts are canceled is near" (Dt 15:8-9).

The laws thus challenge the economic system, question it,
modify it, try to free people from the stranglehold it may have
on them.

Systems, of course, are terribly strong. They reassert themselves
in spite of such official challenge. In Israel the rich managed to
circumvent these laws in the course of time, as we can see from
Amos' vehement protests. One strategy was to make the laws part
of the system by incorporating them as exceptions. By giving in
on some minor points, the rich could maintain their privileged
position and their exploitative practices as before. It is only in
the New Testament that Jesus implemented the full meaning of
the laws by his total reversal of economic values: Not the rich
but the poor are happy; instead of enlarging our property, Jesus
advises us to sell all our belongings and give the money to the
poor; we should lay up riches in heaven; the man who puts his
security in property is simply called a fool; the two copper coins
offered by the poor widow are worth more than the gold and silver
donated by wealthy benefactors. This is where the old economic

system breaks down and a new freedom is born. But the old laws prepared the ground.

Jesus teaches:

> "When someone asks you for something, give it to him;
> When someone wants to borrow something, lend it to him"
> (Mt 5:42).

He is actually quoting the law of Deuteronomy 15:1-11. The essence of that law is having mercy, being generous, being prepared to cancel debts. Jesus incorporated the law into the charter of his kingdom, thereby fulfilling its real purpose of cracking open the system established on wealth as the highest value. We see a similar process in the area of religion.

Overthrow of Pay-off Piety

In the Ancient Middle East, people venerated the powers of nature. According to the most prevalent mythologies, the original father god, El, was no longer in complete control. One of the younger gods, the god of lightning and storm, had obtained the kingship by defeating other gods, such as the sea (Yamm) and death (Moth). This ruling god was variously known as Baal (lord), Melek (king) or Marduk. His wife, a fertility goddess, bore the name Astarte, Asherah or Anath. It was thought that these deities were specially present in their idols, worshipped in shrines and temples. Procuring prosperity and fertility became a system of sacred practices and rites. If one brought the right sacrifices at the right time and in the prescribed manner, the god or goddess would dispense blessings. Faithfulness to the system insured rain for the crops, healthy children, fertile lifestock, protection from disaster. The gods and goddesses were part of the system. They acted in a predictable way.

The great religious innovation of the Old Testament religion was the determined effort to dismantle this system of gods and goddesses. To begin with: God is only one. He is not part of a pantheon of divinities. And on no account can he be captured in an image or an idol.

> "Do not make for yourself images of anything in heaven
> or on earth or in the water under the earth. Do not bow
> down to any idol or worship it, for I am the LORD your God
> and I tolerate no rivals" (Dt 5:8-9).

"Do not sin by making for yourselves an idol in any form at all—whether man or woman, animal or bird, reptile or fish. Do not be tempted to worship and serve what you see in the sky— the sun, the moon and the stars" (Dt 4:16-19).

"Obey his command not to make yourselves any kind of idol, because the Lord your God is like a flaming fire; he tolerates no rivals" (Dt 4:23-24).

It was a commandment which the Israelites would find extremely hard to obey. From the historical books we learn that until the destruction of Jerusalem in 587 the worship of idols continued in many forms. At times the old Canaanitic or Mesopotamian fertility gods were invoked. At times Yahweh himself was represented by an image, as in the golden calves of Bethel and Dan. When King Josiah purified the Temple at Jerusalem, he removed idols representing Baal, Kemosh, Melek, Marduk and Asherah, as well as horses dedicated to the sun. All this, mind you, in God's own Temple! The inclination to represent divinity in a tangible form and to rely on ritual for obtaining blessings was deep-seated indeed.

In our present-day spirit of dialogue and tolerance we might argue: Why not allow people to have something visual to focus their devotion on? Don't we also use statues today, say of the Good Shepherd or the Sacred Heart? Was it really necessary to forbid images and statues in such a radical manner?

The answer lies precisely in the need to demolish the religious system enshrined in statues and idols. God is not part of this world; he is its creator. He is not a power of nature; he transcends it. He does not act in a predictable manner; instead, he changes the course of history by choosing Israel, by liberating them from Egypt and by giving them their own land. God is not male or female. He does not marry or have children. Yet he is a person who shows love and mercy and demands loyalty in return. The system of idols and rituals is replaced by a living covenant in which both God and the people promise mutual love and generosity.

"You saw how I carried you as an eagle carries her young on her wings, and brought you here to me....The whole earth is mine, but you will be my chosen people" (Ex 19:4-5).

"The LORD—and the LORD alone—is our God. Love the LORD your God with all your heart, with all your soul, and with all your strength" (Dt 6:4-5).

To realize this new relationship the old system had to be demolished. The law prescribes this in no uncertain terms:

> "Tear down their altars and smash their sacred stone pillars to pieces. Burn their symbols of the goddess Asherah and chop down their idols" (Dt 12:3).

The system had to go to make place for faith in the living God.

The sad fact is that here, too, as in the economic order, the Israelites gradually turned their allegiance to Yahweh into a new system. The idea of a living covenant with its obligation of genuine love and true sanctity made way for a ritualism in which God was expected to give blessings in return for sacrifices.

> "Do you think I want all these sacrifices you keep offering to me? I have had more than enough of the sheep you burn as sacrifices and of the fat of your fine animals. I am tired of the blood of bulls and sheep and goats. Who asked you to bring me all this when you come to worship me? Who asked you to do all this tramping around in my Temple? It's useless to bring your offerings. I am disgusted with the smell of the incense you burn. I cannot stand your New Moon Festivals, your Sabbaths, and your religious gatherings; they are all corrupted by your sins" (Is 1:11-13).

These prophetic complaints had little effect. It was only when Jesus came that the new system of ritualistic piety was abolished. With Jesus' death on the hill of execution outside Jerusalem a new covenant came into being of a totally different nature.

> "The time is coming and is already here, when by the power of God's Spirit people will worship the Father as he really is, offering him the true worship that he wants. God is spirit, and only by the power of his Spirit can people worship him as he really is" (Jn 4:23-24).

With the coming of the Spirit, direct relationship between God and man has been established. The law of love, infused by the Spirit and consisting of intimate union with Christ Jesus, has freed us from any system. For systems only result in sin and death. The objective of the ancient religious laws, namely, to demolish the religious system has thereby been achieved and human kind finally made free.

Unshackling Day of Leisure

Freedom was also the main purpose of the Sabbath law. The worries of living could all too easily absorb a person's total existence. Again we encounter the clutches of a system, in this case the system of daily routine, stereotype duties, inward-looking activity. The Sabbath offered a way out. It forced men and women to pause and rest, to have time for leisure and reflection, to become aware of wider realities.

> "You have six days in which to do your work, but the seventh day is a day of rest, dedicated to me. On that day no one is to work—neither you, your children, your slaves, your animals, nor the foreigners who live in your country. Your slaves must rest just as you do" (Dt 5:13-14).

Notice that the purpose of the law is not to enjoin religious worship on that day. Nowhere do we find it stated that work is forbidden to give people time to attend services or to say prayers. No, the law prescribes the rest itself, the leisure, the being free from the usual grind of work and worry. The rest was required because humanity is bigger than work, just as God is bigger than his role as creator. God finished creation in six days, we are told.

> "He blessed the seventh day and set it apart as a special day, because by that day he had completed his creation and stopped working" (Gn 2:3).

Men and women, who are true persons created as images of God himself, express their free, god-like origin by enjoying leisure.

Do I need to repeat it again? The Sabbath itself became yet another system, the very opposite of what it was meant to be. When the priests and scribes got their hands on it, they turned it into a duty, an obligation, a condition for blessing. I shudder when I read, "Whoever does not keep it [the day of rest], but works on that day, is to be put to death" (Ex 31:14). It was the first step to the unbelievable legalism that was to be showered on keeping the Sabbath. In Jesus' time what was meant to be a day of joy and leisure had been turned into a day of horror and mental paralysis. One could hardly move without fear of infringing the law. Small wonder that Jesus fought this interpretation of the Sabbath: "The Sabbath was made for the good of man; man was not made for the Sabbath" (Mk 2:27). And this applies to all laws.

Revolutionary Liberty

It is clear from the foregoing that I am suggesting a different way of reading the Old Testament laws. We can, of course, read them in isolation and reflect on the values they contain. But much more profitably, I believe, we should meditate on them against the whole background of God's history of salvation. We know that it was God's intention to make us truly free, to remove any obstacle between God and ourselves, to create a new relationship entirely based on mutual love and not on a system of laws. In the light of this divine plan we can see how he gradually opened the way to a realization of this new order. We can see how God compelled the Israelites to think and behave in a way contrary to the systems by which they were enslaved. We notice that the old systems constantly reassert themselves, that they reappear in the guise of modified and corrected versions. We observe with dismay that legalism and ritualism, an enslavement in systems, gained the upper hand in the Jewish practice of religion in later times.

But then, we know, Jesus entered the scene and he overturned all those systems. His Sermon on the Mount is a calculated and deliberate departure from the approach followed by the Jewish leaders of his time. It is a return to God's original intention, but in a far more radical manner. Every single example Jesus gives of the new conduct expected in his kingdom defies incorporation into a system. Being spiritually poor, desiring God's justice, showing mercy, working for peace, enduring persecution, being the salt of the earth and light of the world, giving your coat to whoever takes your shirt—these indicate attitudes that transcend and defy exact legislation. But these attitudes were present in a seminal form in the old system-destroying laws. These laws, therefore, retain their use as the starting point of God's program of instruction.

Studying the Old Testament laws in this way is also necessary because it may open our eyes to our own relapses into a slavery to systems. We find in the history of the church, just as in the Israelite kingdoms, a constant inclination for people to turn Christian practice into systems of one sort or another. For many centuries Christians thought that the capitalist system was officially sanctioned by God. They quoted laws from scripture and canon law to support this view, which included the right to capture slaves, possess them, buy them and sell them. The encyclicals of one pope after another have now dislodged this false support of a particular economic system. Vatican II expressed it in official church teaching. But the facts of history prove that for centuries the system held people in its grasp.

Even now there are Catholics who consider the whole church in terms of a system of organizational structures and laws defining everyone's rights and duties. Without realizing it, they go against the very nature of what God and Jesus intended. The ministries in the church have authority and power, but they are meant to liberate and heal, not to enslave. The laws of the kingdom are meant to create freedom, not to curtail it. For a Christian there should be no such thing as feeling safe when working within the system. We are the people of God. Jesus is present to us in many exciting ways: in his word; in his ministers who serve and guide us; in his sacramental signs; in the fellowship of love; in his Spirit which shines through all these realities.

Everyday realities — they are the test case of every law. What was more commonplace than seeing a man struggling with his donkey? What to do about it, if you didn't like that man?

> "If you happen to see your enemy's cow or donkey running loose, take it back to him. If his donkey has fallen under its load, help him get the donkey to its feet again; don't just walk off" (Ex 23:4-5).

Walking off with ill-disguised glee is exactly what our human system of helping only our friends would have us do. Helping someone whom we distrust or dislike breaks through that system. It is as unusual and unpredictable as doing good to those who hate you, blessing people who curse you, praying for those who ill-treat you! This falls outside any system; it cannot be formulated in any law.

> The Spirit produces love, joy, peace, patience, kindness, goodness, faithfulness, humility, and self-control. There is no law against such things as these (Gal 5:22-23).
>
> If the Spirit leads you, then you are not subject to the Law (Gal 5:18).
>
> For the whole Law is summed up in one commandment: "Love your neighbor as you love yourself" (Gal 5:14).

18

A Royal Envoy
That Was Spat Upon

I knew a sister who in her congregation had been a real peacemaker. Before she became Provincial, the communities of the province had been torn by division and conflicts. Through her skill as a leader and by her personal example she had succeeded in bringing back peace and harmony to her congregation.

"It must be a great satisfaction to you to know you are a peacemaker," I said. "Jesus said: 'Blessed are the peacemakers, for they shall see God.' "

"Yes, I am happy that peace has been restored," she said, "but nobody realizes, I am sure, what it cost me in nerves and personal humiliation."

"What do you mean?" I asked.

"When I began this office, I started with a lot of enthusiasm and idealism. I saw that I was called to an important task. Somehow or other I understood that God wanted me for a special reason, namely, for this work of reconciliation. But I had not realized that it couldn't be done without a lot of personal involvement and personal suffering. I can't tell you how often I felt lonely and rejected by other sisters. It is only gradually that I have come to understand that the ministry of reconciliation cannot be brought about without personal cost."

Many of us, I believe, have to go through a similar development in our vocation. It is interesting in this context to see how the same insight, the same gradual discovery of all the implications in the ministry of reconciliation, can be found within the prophecies of the book of Isaiah. Isaiah, too, was full of enthusiasm at the beginning of his ministry. He knew that God intended him to bring his people back.

> The LORD says, "Now let's settle the matter. You are
> stained red with sin, but I will wash you as clean as snow.
> Although your stains are deep red you will be as white as
> wool" (Is 1:18).

When Isaiah received his call, he was praying in the Temple.
I imagine that he was kneeling down in the court of Israel facing
the high altar that stood just before the actual inner Temple
building. Suddenly in his mind's eye he saw that the whole Temple was filled with God's glory. And right above everything else
he saw a throne of God. God himself was sitting on it as a king
in the middle of his palace.

> I saw the LORD. He was sitting on his throne high and ex-
> alted, and his robe filled the whole Temple. Round him flam-
> ing creatures were standing, each of which had six wings.
> Each creature covered its face with two wings, and its body
> with two, and used the other two for flying. They were call-
> ing out to each other:
> "Holy, holy, holy!
> The LORD Almighty is holy!
> His glory fills the world" (Is 6:1-3).

Isaiah then heard that he was called to purify himself from his
sins. An angel came down picked up a burning coal from the altar
and cleansed his lips with it. Then he was, as it were, admitted
into God's own court. He heard God explained through his angels
how he had tried in vain to bring the people of Israel to repentance. "What else can I do?" God asked. Some of the angels advised God to bring even more punishment on the people. "Send
them another famine," one of them said, "then they will surely
change their minds." When Isaiah heard this discussion, he felt
a great zeal for God's holiness and also compassion with his own
people. In a sincere moment of enthusiasm he volunteered to
become God's envoy.

> Then I heard the LORD say, "Whom shall I send? Who will
> be our messenger?"
> I answered, "I will go! Send me!" (Is 6:8).

Thus Isaiah began his prophetic mission. It was a demanding
task, but at the same time a glorious career. What a challenge
to go out in the public streets and meet the king himself face to
face with a threatening oracle from God!

"Ask the LORD your God to give you a sign. It can be from
deep in the world of the dead or from high up in heaven"
(Is 7:11).

It was a task that had with it the glamour of being a represen-
tative of the highest authority in the universe, the most powerful emperor, the King of Kings! Isaiah in this way fulfilled his
mission as many of us, I am sure, imagine we will fulfill our
ministry of reconciliation. I call this particular stage of our
ministry the royal phase. It gives us courage and strength. But
if we remain in this phase without further growth, we are in
danger of becoming career prophets.

The Strength of Meekness

Isaiah, we know, lived in the 8th century B.C. But his prophecies did not die with him. After his death Isaiah's disciples continued to meditate on the meaning of his life and his words. This
was particularly important when Jerusalem was destroyed and
the people of Judah taken into exile in 586 B.C. Isaiah's disciples
took the prophecies with them and reflected on their meaning
in the context of these new experiences. A very remarkable and
important new interpretation arose.

The Jews who lived in exile were, of necessity, reduced to pover-
ty and to a status of subjection. Wherever they were, they may
have had to perform menial tasks. They became a minority
tolerated by others, but not greatly esteemed. This experience of
their new, humble status brought about also the insight that
God's ministry of reconciliation could profitably, and perhaps
more effectively, be exercised from within such a condition. The
so-called servant prophecies express this very convincingly.

We don't know for certain whether these servant prophecies
refer to one individual. But I believe it to be so. It seems to me
that one of the disciples of Isaiah received a special call from God
to be a leader among his friends and that he saw himself in a
new role, called upon to realize again Isaiah's ministry, but in
a new fashion. He knew that God had called him to be his servant, that God had chosen him and was pleased with him. What
was new in the self-understanding of this Deutero-Isaiah was the
realization that God had called him not to a glorious and
glamorous ministry but to a ministry of gentle and humble
service.

> He will not shout or raise his voice
>   or make loud speeches in the streets.
> He will not break off a bent reed
>   nor put out a flickering lamp.
> He will bring lasting justice to all
> He will not lose hope or courage;
>   he will establish justice on the earth (Is 42:2-4).

Whereas the original Isaiah had been raising his voice in the public streets and had been shouting a message of warning and future punishment, the new servant was called upon to bring God's justice through a life of gentleness and service. This mission, though exercised in a more humble fashion, was not less ambitious. In fact, whereas Isaiah had only preached God's message to his own people, Deutero-Isaiah knew God wanted him to bring salvation also to the other nations in the world.

> "I have a greater task for you, my servant.
>   Not only will you restore to greatness
>   the people of Israel who have survived,
> but I will also make you a light to the nations—
>   so that all the world may be saved" (Is 49:6).

The implications of this insight are of great value. The weight of the ministry has now shifted from conveying a royal message to expressing that message of salvation in one's own life situation. This becomes even clearer when the person of the prophet is seen to be used by God as an instrument expressing God's will to save.

> The LORD has given me understanding,
>   and I have not rebelled
>   or turned away from him.
> I bared my back to those who beat me
>   I did not stop them when they insulted me,
>   when they pulled out the hairs of my beard
>   and spit in my face (Is 50:5-6).

The Success of Suffering

I imagine that this particular person, Deutero-Isaiah, did undergo persecution. If the information we find is correct, he may have been falsely accused and put to death by a Babylonian court. His disciples were at first completely taken aback, but later they realized that through these events their master had realized the mission to which he knew himself called. Under the light of further inspiration, they expressed their conviction that their master's suffering was the instrument God used to bring forgiveness and reconciliation to many. They were also convinced that on account of this vicarious suffering, their master would receive a very high reward from God. These convictions are expressed in the well-known Song of the Suffering Servant (Isaiah 52:13—53:12). It was a breakthrough in Old Testament theology, for in that song the function of vicarious suffering, in fact the use of suffering at all, is expressed for the first time in very clear terms:

"But he endured the suffering that should have been ours,
    the pain that we should have borne.
All the while we thought that his suffering
    was punishment sent by God.
But because of our sins he was wounded,
    beaten because of the evil we did.
We are healed by the punishment he suffered,
    made whole by the blows he received" (Is 53:4-5).

We can see the implication of this new discovery for our own ministry. We too need to realize that God may have a different way of looking at our ministry than we do. Where we might be inclined to stress the aspect of external proclamation and mediation, God would seem to be inclined to give greater weight to the gift of our personality and the cost we are prepared to pay in his service. Thus the paradox of ministry arises. What may seem to result in pain and failure may turn out to be a very fruitful ministry in God's eyes. The results which God reaps from our efforts may lie on an entirely different plane from what we expected. When we begin to realize this, our ministry enters the phase of the suffering servant.

This may prove a great consolation to us. The frustration and humiliation which necessarily will come our way, if we give ourselves wholeheartedly to God's service, may turn out to be, perhaps, the most valuable part of our ministry. It may be that we ourselves will not see the immediate outcome of our efforts. It may be that our contribution will not be recognized by others. It may be that for all practical purposes our life will end in death before we have achieved anything in terms of external success. But for God it may have been a very fruitful and successful mission. God's logic is different from ours. And we know it.

The prophecy of the suffering servant, though revealing the fruit of failure and pointing to future reward and exaltation, was not yet the full picture of the ministry intended by God. We find this expressed in a further re-working of the prophecies in the school of Isaiah in later centuries. It gave rise to the prophecies of Trito-Isaiah. In this last stage there is a greater awareness of the ultimate victory, of the joy and liberation that will come when God brings actual salvation. The prophet now realizes that, even though his ministry will be filled with frustration and suffering, it will also bring with it the consolation of true joy and visible happiness.

> The Sovereign LORD has filled me with his spirit.
> He has chosen me and sent me
> To bring good news to the poor,
> To heal the broken-hearted,
> To announce release to captives
> And freedom to those in prison....
> To give to those who mourn in Zion
> Joy and gladness instead of grief,
> A song of praise instead of sorrow (Is 61:1,3).

We have now reached the deepest insight in the ministry. It is God's Spirit that makes it possible for us to work for his purpose and speak in God's name. It is that same Spirit who gave us divine authorization and made us true royal envoys. It is that same Spirit who gives us the strength to carry our sufferings and to understand our apparent failures. But the very same Spirit will also fill our hearts with joy at the happy tidings of liberation which we will be allowed to bring. There is, therefore, in this latest phase, the phase of God's Spirit, a fuller awareness of redemption and victory. In our ministry we too will be granted this privilege if we sincerely dedicate ourselves to our mission. After the initial glamour has worn off, after we will have been allowed to drink from the cup of suffering and rejection, God will also anoint us with the oil of gladness. We will in ways beyond our own understanding be allowed to see that our work brings true happiness to people, that our healing binds up wounds, that our touch brings comfort where there had been sorrow and division. It is at this stage that we will truly experience how God's Spirit works through us. No longer will our mission be seen as something we do, as something external to us. We will then really experience how God's Spirit is making use of our total selves, of the pains of our body and the feelings of our hearts, in his service of peace and reconciliation.

"Learn From Me"

Jesus Christ himself was aware of these different aspects or phases in his ministry. We see him quote the various texts I have referred to so far. Are we allowed to uncover in the gospel traces of his own mental and spiritual development? Would it be so impossible to imagine that Jesus, too, volunteered as Isaiah had done before him by saying to his Father: "Here I am. Send me"? Are we entirely wrong to think that Jesus too, though theoretically aware of the possibility of suffering, only gradually experienced it as a hard reality by the opposition of the Pharisees and scribes? Could it be that Jesus also, like ourselves, was granted by his Father the joy and happiness of seeing his mission anointed by the fruits of the Spirit? In other words: Could it be that going through these various phases of our calling is a natural growth that should take part in everyone who is serving God as Jesus did?

I find the book of Isaiah a marvelous record of the different aspects and experiences of being a prophet. The early Isaiah shows zeal and idealism. His participation in the glory of the divine majesty remains as a true element of vocation. Next to it, however, and as a further fulfillment of it, the lonely struggles and sufferings of the servant are clearly depicted. This is another element that should never be forgotten. Finally, the consolation of bringing joy and healing are expressed without diminishing in any way what was said in previous prophecies. This juxtaposition also gives us matter for thought. In our own lives we should do a continuous re-reading of our own convictions and ideals. While acknowledging the reality and value of our earlier ideals, we should be prepared to enrich them constantly by new experiences and further growth. God is our Father who gradually draws us closer to himself. He allows us to be ourselves at every moment of our development. He does not deny our past, but calls us ever to greater depths of realization and greater heights of participation in his own being. Every day we should be prepared to learn. "Every morning he makes me eager to hear what he is going to teach me" (Is 50:4). For God is continuously doing unexpected and exciting things. "Now I will tell you of new things to come, events that I did not reveal before" (Is 48:6). Is it not wonderful to serve such a God?

19

The Word That Makes
People a People

Moses was told by God to bring the Hebrews out of Egypt. He was to confront the pharaoh with the repeated divine command: "Let my people go, that they may serve me!" An early oracle puts it this way:

> "Israel is my first-born son. I told you to let my son go, so that he might worship me, but you refused. Now I am going to kill your first-born son" (Ex 4:22-23).

In this oracle the people are spoken of as one person: God's first-born son. The reason is partly the prophet's desire to contrast Israel with the pharaoh's eldest son. But it shows at the same time that the whole people were thought of as a single entity. They were looked upon as one community.

This can also be seen in the way God concluded his covenant with the people. He made his offer to all of them as one community.

> "You saw what I, the LORD did to the Egyptians and how I carried you as an eagle carries her young on her wings, and brought you here to me. Now, if you will obey me and keep my covenant, you will be my own people. The whole earth is mine, but you will be my chosen people, a people dedicated to me alone" (Ex 19:4-6).

By offering them the covenant, God gave the people a new beginning. In fact, through the covenant they became a new community, his community. It was his word that made them the community they were. God created them as a community through his word.

> "Listen now, Israel my servant,
>   my chosen people, the descendants of Jacob.

177

> I am the LORD who created you;
>   from the time you were born I have helped you.
> Do not be afraid; you are my servant,
>   my chosen people whom I love" (Is 44:1-2).
> Israel, the LORD who created you says,
> "Do not be afraid—I will save you.
> I have called you by name—you are mine" (Is 43:1).

As God created the universe by commanding "Let there be light," "Let there by a sky," "Let there be dry land," so he created Israel through the word of his covenant.

You may wonder why I am reflecting on this aspect of God's word. The reason is that in our approach to faith and in our spiritual life, we have become very individualistic. We have become very much aware of the value of God's word for our personal, spiritual good. We read scripture as a word addressed to us personally, and we draw conclusions for our own life. Now there is nothing wrong in this, as long as we do not forget the community-creating function of scripture. The Ethiopian official who was on his way to Gaza was reading excerpts of Deutero-Isaiah. It became the starting point for his conversion and baptism (Acts 8:26-40). The Bible is indeed God's word to individuals, but it can and should do more.

The Sacramental Word

It may be useful to review some of the major trends in scriptural spirituality that the church has experienced through the centuries. As I will be condensing very complex movements in just a few sentences, I will, of necessity, oversimplify the presentation. But simple presentations also have their uses. Like caricatures, they may bring out more clearly the salient points. What we are interested in here is understanding how the spirituality which we live can influence our way of reading scripture.

The first stream of spirituality I would like to sketch is what I would like to call *the spirituality of sacral realities*. In this spirituality, the greatest emphasis is placed on the holiness of God, on his being altogether different and sacred. God's holiness came among us when God's Son assumed a human nature. God's holiness permeates the church in such sacred realities as the sacraments, ordained ministers, canon law and ancient traditions.

The closer that Christians moved to these sacred realities, the closer they were to God. Sacred Scripture was seen to be one of these holy realities, and so its sanctifying power was highly appreciated. But, note well, its power was, somehow or other, an external sacramental contact rather than a word or a message.

Perhaps I should be more specific and describe this spirituality in a concrete instance. The European Middle Ages expressed their awe and worship through their beautiful Gothic cathedrals. These buildings themselves are like a prayer. They established a sacred reality in the middle of people's cities and towns. Within these churches the history of salvation was made visual through sculptures, mural paintings and stained-glass windows. Mass was celebrated in solemn liturgies, the priests wearing embroidered vestments and using plenty of incense. The ordinary people who came to pray in these churches became aware of God's presence through the sacred realities they saw. The Bible too would come to them in that way. They had never read the Bible, of course; They probably could not read and write, and even if they could, books were very rare and costly. When the Bible was read out in the liturgy, it was read in Latin, a language they could not understand. The priest might explain its contents in his sermon (which might also be in Latin), but ordinary believers were convinced they did not *need* to know the Bible in that way since its contents were expressed in the church anyway. What they did want was to be blessed by the Bible. At the end of Mass the priest would hold the scroll which had John, chapter one, inscribed on it, while imparting the blessing.

Until about 30 years ago, priests and religious used to recite the breviary in Latin. Many priests could understand the Latin, but some could not; religious lay brothers often had great difficulty about this. I remember one of our professors speaking about this to us when I was a student in the minor seminary:

> You can have true devotion even if you do not follow the meaning of the text. Once-upon-a-time there was a lay brother who had to recite the psalms in Latin, but who did not understand a word of what he was saying. So he prayed to God for the gift of Latin. God appeared to him and granted him the gift. But when he started saying the psalms with understanding, he began to be terribly distracted by it. So in the end, he asked God to withdraw the gift. He could pray better without it!

Another example from my own experience:

As recently as 1962 a parish priest I knew in the north of Italy used to make his mass servers recite Lauds in Latin before Mass. "But they don't understand a word of it!" I objected. "That does not matter," he said. "They know these are inspired psalms and the official prayer of the church. God knows what they mean and he will be pleased!"

The Word of Encounter

While this spirituality was still very strong in many traditions of European Christianity, a new spirituality grew up which I would like to characterize as the *spirituality of the meeting between God and the soul*. Not the ornate cathedral with the pomp and splendor of liturgy, but the bare cell or the simple prayer room became the place of experiencing God's presence. The whole stress lay on purifying one's own personality, to embrace Christ in an interior, spiritual union. Sacred Scripture was now seen to fulfill a new role. It was considered to contain the words of Christ, words that should be listened to with great humility and reverence. *The Imitation of Christ* (A.D.1427) expressed this new perception in conversation between Christ and his disciple:

> "My Son," says our Lord, "hear my words and follow them, for they are most sweet, far surpassing the wisdom and learning of all philosophers and all the wise men of the world. My words are spiritual and cannot be apprehended fully by man's intelligence. Neither are they to be adapted or applied according to the vain pleasure of the hearer, but are to be heard in silence, with great humility and reverence, with great inward affection of the heart and in great rest and quiet of body and soul...."
>
> "Speak to me, Lord Jesus. You have the words of eternal life. Speak them to me for the full comfort of my soul and give me amendment of all my past life, to your joy, honour and glory."
>
> *—The Imitation of Christ*, Bk.3, ch. 2-3

Such an approach to scripture obviously requires translations in the vernacular. Through the invention of printing and the influence of the Reformation, scripture became more and more the spiritual guidebook for the individual. This was very much in line with other individualizing trends in society and the church. Democracy, freedom and equality for all and the right to education and personal development all helped to strengthen an individualistic approach to spirituality. Scripture was seen as God's word speaking to the person. Preaching in the liturgy, catechetics and various lay apostolates also stressed the need for the individual way.

Word Founding a Community

Meanwhile, a third spirituality had arisen in the church. This spirituality, which I will call the *spirituality of belonging to God's people*, has gained momentum in the past decade. It has ancient roots in the early Christian communities, in monastic groups, in popular religious movements. Vatican II gave it a new impulse by redefining the church in terms of people rather than structures. The freedom struggles of South American base communities provided the possibility and need of explicit theological formulation. In this movement of thought and spirituality, scripture is experienced as the charter of God's people, creating the community through the word. God's word is not just an intellectual event. It brings about deeds of liberation. It calls for a response from the whole community, in communal sharing and in common action. I am not so much asking, *What is God saying to me individually?*, rather, I am constantly listening to the word as a member of the whole community, wondering what he expects from us as a group.

After this lengthy historical footnote, I would like to return to my original observation: namely, that God's word does, indeed, create community. The most beautiful illustration of this can be found in Nehemiah 8-10 which describes how the reading of God's inspired word made the returned exiles into a new community. I recommend that the passage be read in its entirety. Here I will point out the various community-building aspects that we should pay attention to.

When the exiles had returned to Palestine and settled, they came together in Jerusalem. There they took up the communal reading of God's word:

> "Ezra brought it [the book of the Law] to the place where the people had gathered — men, women, and the children who were old enough to understand. There in the square by the gate he read the Law to them from dawn until noon, and they all listened attentively" (Neh 8:2-3).

The communal character of the reading is further explained. Ezra was assisted by 13 Levites, mentioned by name, who were responsible for different groups of the people, if I understand the text correctly. These Levites had to make sure that the people understood what was read out. "They gave an oral translation of God's Law and explained it so that the people could understand it"(Neh 8:8). The response of the people is then described. At the end of that first day a community feast arose spontaneously:

> All the people went home and ate and drank joyfully and shared what they had with others, because they understood what had been read to them (Neh 8:12).

The common study of the Law continued. People decided to live in tents, as was required for the feast of tabernacles, but which had not been done since the day of Joshua. The festival lasted for seven days. "From the first day of the festival to the last they read a part of God's Law every day" (Neh 8:18).

Three weeks later they assembled once more for a new ceremony. It focused on dealing with the past.

> For about three hours the Law of the LORD their God was read to them, and for the next three hours they confessed their sins and worshiped the LORD their God (Neh 9:3).

From the text that follows it is clear that the event was a community act of reconciliation. Through personal testimonies people acknowledged that they had not been faithful to the covenant and new commitments were made. The prayer of Nehemiah 9:6-37 is an expression of the community's feelings. It theologizes the past and the present in terms of "we, your people." It speaks of the people's problems:"We are slaves in the land that you gave us....we are in deep distress." Even if some individuals played a leading role in the whole process, they spoke on behalf of the people and from their midst.

Finally, the old covenant was renewed by a written undertaking, signed by the heads of the clans and families. It bound the people to a number of social and religious reforms which had been formulated in response to the Law. The document opens with the phrase: "We, the people of Israel...."

It might be worthwhile to examine which function we ascribe to God's word in our own spiritual life. Does the reading of the word in the liturgy make the believers into a community, as it should do? Is there scope for discussion, sharing, a common interpretation of what it means for this group? Does the Word of God lead to a collective response of the community? Have we ourselves learned, and taught others, how the Word of God can make us his people?

20

Storing Treasures
That Rapture the Mind

We usually think of Jesus as a kind and gentle person. And rightly so. Yet on one occasion he was consumed with holy anger. That was the day when he cleared the Temple square of merchants and marketeers. He made a whip from cords. He drove cattle and sheep out of the Temple. He overturned the tables of the moneychangers and ordered the men who sold pigeons, "Get out of here!" Single-handed he chased them out. No one could resist the power of his determination.

Why was Jesus so furious? What had aroused his anger? He said: "It is written in the Scriptures that God said, 'My Temple will be called a house of prayer for the people of all nations' " (Mk 11:17). Notice the stress on "the people of all nations." The buying and selling was not going on in the inner courts — the court of women and the court of Israel — where the Jews offered their prayers. The market tents had been set up in the outer court, the court for the Gentiles, the non-Jews. Foreigners who came to pray in the Temple were not allowed to enter the inner courts. They could only pray in this place — a square which had now been turned into a marketplace!

Jesus was angry because non-Jews could not say their prayers peacefully. He felt this so deeply because God had specifically promised that non-Jews who joined the covenant would not be treated as second-class citizens. Listen to these words from the book of Isaiah.

> A foreigner who has joined the LORD's people should not say, "The LORD will not let me worship with his people...." The LORD says to such a man, "If you honor me by observing the Sabbath and if you do what pleases me and faithfully keep my covenant, then your name will be remembered in

my Temple and among my people longer than if you had
sons and daughters. You will never be forgotten....I will
bring you to Zion my sacred hill, give you joy in my house
of prayer, and accept the sacrifices you offer on my altar.
My Temple will be called a house of prayer for the people
of all nations" (Is 56:3,4-5,7).

This was a beautiful reassurance. Jesus was angry because the
business going on in the Temple belied God's promise. The court
for the foreigners was no longer a place dedicated to prayer. It
had been turned into a "hideout for thieves."

Jesus' Spiritual Depository

Let us consider the incident carefully. First of all, from a reading
of the text in Isaiah we can see that the short line which Jesus
quoted, "My house will be called a house of prayer," is truly the
heart of the whole passage. To understand what Jesus meant with
the quotation we have to know the *whole* Old Testament passage.
This often applies to short quotations in Jesus' words. Usually
we have to study the complete scripture passage to which Jesus
is referring.

Another thing we notice is that Jesus was familiar with the text
of Isaiah, that is, when Jesus came across the market scene in
the court of the Gentiles he did not have the time or the opportunity to study the scriptures. No, seeing what was going on, he
remembered the promise in Isaiah. Immediately he realized the
contrast between what God was saying in Isaiah and what was
actually happening in the Temple. Seeing that contrast made him
angry! So we know from this that Jesus knew the Isaian text by
heart, that it was one of the scripture passages dear to him.

How did Jesus learn scripture? In his days no one could afford
to possess private copies of the Old Testament books. People
learned the text because on every Sabbath a portion of Torah, the
Pentateuch, and selections from the prophets would be read out.
The reading was done from the Hebrew text with free translations in Aramaic. That is where Jesus learned the Old Testament
passages. At times he, like other members of the community, may
have been called upon to do the reading. He may also have stayed
behind in the synagogue after the service was over to do some
private reading and study. But he did not make any notes, nor
did he have his own collection of bible scrolls.

When Jesus heard a particular text that struck him as being important, he would memorize as much as he could. People were much more used to doing this than we are. He would then reflect on the passage in the course of the week and work out its implications for his kingdom. During the years Jesus spent in Nazareth he built up in this manner a "treasury," a mental storeroom, of important scripture texts. They were his own selection of texts, and he gave them his own interpretation. We can be certain of this, because when he started his public ministry, we find him making use of this treasury of Old Testament texts.

Jesus actually refers to this when talking to the apostles:

> "This means, then, that every teacher of the Law who becomes a disciple in the Kingdom of heaven is like a homeowner who takes new and old things out of his storage room" (Mt 13:52).

The teacher in Christ's kingdom has many old treasures in his storeroom. But they turn out also to be new because of the new understanding he imparts to them.

Jesus' example shows us how to derive the most benefit from scripture. Even though we are now privileged to have the whole printed text continuously at our disposal, we, too, cannot possess the whole Bible at once. Not all texts will be equally telling to us. So we too should build up a treasury, a storeroom of select passages that are dear to us. Whenever a text has made a deep impression on us, when we have reflected on it and somehow made it our own, we add it to our selection. That is a very good way of gradually assembling our own collection of "gems" from scripture. We can do this by noting these texts in a special "treasury booklet" or by marking the passages in our bible.

Creative Interpretation

After this useful diversion, let's return to Jesus' cleansing of the Temple. We saw that he was angry because non-Jews, foreigners, could not pray in the Temple in accordance with God's promise. This brings me to another observation. The Old Testament was full of prejudice against non-Jews. Only the Israelites were God's chosen people. Especially in the older sections of the Bible God almost appears to be irrationally partial. He always favored the Jews and was biased against foreigners.

Isaiah 56:1-8 — in which God says foreigners are welcome in his Temple — was selected by Jesus precisely because it heralded a new approach. It is clear from the gospels that Jesus felt no prejudice against other nations. The Roman officer and the Syro-Phoenician woman are held out as model believers. Jesus stayed in a Samaritan village and said his Father would accept true worship from anyone. Samaritans also appear as examples of neighborly charity and gratitude. Jesus, therefore, strongly believed that all people from all nations should belong to his kingdom. That is why Jesus rejected the Old Testament texts that betray a pro-Jewish bias and gave special prominence to the promise of salvation to all.

If we keep this concern of Jesus in mind we also understand the original way in which he could handle the Old Testament. Isaiah 23:1-18, for instance, contains a condemnation of Tyre and Sidon, the two wealthy merchant cities north of Palestine. It announces punishment and destruction.

> Howl with grief, you people of Phoenicia!...The Lord has stretched out his hand over the sea and overthrown kingdoms. He has ordered the Phoenician centers of commerce to be destroyed. City of Sidon, your happiness has ended (Is 23:6,11-12).

The Jews knew this prophecy well. Perhaps they discussed among themselves when God would execute this judgement. Jesus too had reflected on the prophecy. But he understood that in it God condemned Tyre and Sidon for their sins and unbelief, not because they were not part of the chosen people. That is why Jesus can turn the prophecy against the Jews themselves:

> "How terrible it will be for you, Chorazin! How terrible for you too, Bethsaida! If the miracles which were performed in you had been performed in Tyre and Sidon, the people there would long ago have put on sackcloth and sprinkled ashes on themselves, to show that they had turned from their sins! I assure you that on the Judgment Day God will show more mercy to the people of Tyre and Sidon than to you" (Mt 11:21-22).

In another Isaian prophecy God describes how he will humiliate the pride of the king of Babylonia.

> King of Babylon, bright morning star, you have fallen from heaven....You said you would climb to the tops of the clouds

and be like the Almighty. But instead, you have been brought down to the deepest part of the world of the dead (Is 14:12,14-15).

Jesus applied this text to the town of Capernaum.

"And as for you, Capernaum! Did you want to lift yourself up to heaven? You will be thrown down to hell! If the miracles which were performed in you had been performed in Sodom, it would still be in existence today! You can be sure that on the Judgment Day God will show more mercy to Sodom than to you!" (Mt 11:23-24).

Jesus reproaches his contemporaries for their unbelief. At the same time he underlines that God will judge all nations equally.

Jesus shows the same preoccupation in the parable of the vineyard. The owner rents it out, but the tenants refuse to pay the share of the harvest they owe him. Eventually the owner sends his own son, whom they decide to kill. The parable clearly points to Israel, for according to Isaiah 5:1-7, Israel was God's vineyard.

"Israel is the vineyard of the LORD Almighty;
the people of Judah are the vines he planted.
He expected them to do what was good,
but instead they committed murder" (Is 5:7).

The Son, sent by the owner as a last attempt "at least they will respect my son," points to Jesus himself. Jesus gave an outline, therefore, of salvation history which the Jews would apply to themselves.

But then Jesus introduced a new element. In the Isaian prophecy God had announced punishment: Wild animals would eat the vines and trample them down, the vineyard would be overgrown with weeds, no rain would fall, etc. Jesus brings his audience to another conclusion.

"Now, when the owner of that vineyard comes, what will he do to those tenants?" Jesus asked.

"He will certainly kill those evil men," they answered, "and rent the vineyard out to other tenants, who will give him his share of the harvest at the right time." "And so I tell you," said Jesus, "the Kingdom of God will be taken away from you and given to a people who will produce the proper fruits" (Mt 21:40-41,43).

The kingdom of God will be taken away from Israel and given to believers of other nations who will produce the proper fruits. This was a new development not foreseen in Isaiah 5:1-7 and not suspected by the Jews, but clear to Jesus. His kingdom would cover the whole world and not just the Jewish people.

Jesus found a confirmation of this wider vision in another Isaian oracle which he certainly applied to himself. It began:

> The LORD says,
> "Here is my servant, whom I strengthen—
> the one I have chosen; with whom I am pleased.
> I have filled him with my spirit,
> and he will bring justice to every nation" (Is 42:1).

It was this text which dominated Jesus' thinking during his baptism in the Jordan, and when he had his ecstasy on the mountain. He was conscious of this text while exercising his healing ministry (Mt 12:15-21). In a manner of speaking, Isaiah 42 expressed the way Jesus conceived his own vocation. And the universality of his mission was clearly contained in that oracle:

> "He will bring justice to every nation" (v. 1).
> "Distant lands eagerly wait for his teaching" (v. 4).

And especially,

> "Through you I will make a covenant with all peoples;
> through you I will bring light to the nations" (v. 6).

Jesus knew that his mission extended far beyond the narrow confines of Palestine.

Conclusion

Let us recapitulate what we have seen regarding Jesus' way of studying the Old Testament. He selected certain passages which he found particularly meaningful for reflection and prayer. These he stored in his memory as a precious collection he could draw from. He used texts often in a new form, interpreting them in the new light that came from his kingdom.

The apostles learned from Jesus the same creative approach to scripture. The Isaian and Deutero-Isaian texts Jesus applied to himself were now understood in their full redemptive teaching. Jesus' openness to non-Jews was now expressed in deeds: in suppressing the Mosaic laws that would hinder the conversion of those not familiar with the Jewish past (Acts 15). This is how

Jesus wanted it to be. He wanted the word to be like a seed — ever growing to maturity and producing marvelous fruits.

We too should approach scripture in this way. We should build up a collection of favorite texts. And we should always be prepared to make the word speak to us with a new message in a new situation. For the word creates life:

"My word is like the snow and the rain
  that come down from the sky to water the earth.
They make the crops grow
  and provide seed for planting and food to eat.
So also will be the word that I speak —
  it will not fail to do what I plan for it;
  it will do everything I send it to do" (Is 55:10-11).